Restoring
THE
FALLEN

CREATING SAFE SPACES
FOR THOSE WHO FAIL

MARK & CHERITH STIBBE

malcolm down

PUBLISHING

23 22 21 20 19   7 6 5 4 3 2 1

First published 2019 by Malcolm Down Publishing Ltd.
www.malcolmdown.co.uk

British Library Cataloguing in Publication Data
A catalogue record for this book is available from the British Library.

ISBN 978-1-912863-07-5

Cover design by Esther Kotecha
Art direction by Sarah Grace
Printed in the UK by Bell & Bain Ltd, Glasgow

DEDICATION

We dedicate this book to John and Margaret Parkin, whose
healing influence on both of our lives can never be measured
in the frailty of human words.
Thank you.

And to our beloved Ginny Cryer, who went to be with the
Lord shortly before the publication of this book.
Home at last.

CONTENTS

ACKNOWLEDGEMENTS

To all those whose names we've mentioned in this book, many of whom have written endorsements for us, we want to express our undying thanks and our fondest love. Without you, we would be wandering aimlessly and listlessly in the 'far country'. Thanks to you, we are home again, in the presence of a good, good Father.

FOREWORD (1)

It was around ten years ago that I was finally introduced to my Father. My heavenly Father, that is.

I had been saved at the age of 8 in a 'Come Together' meeting. I was baptised in water and the Holy Spirit and I loved God. I spent the next part of my life serving in Church, worshipping, growing and learning. But it wasn't until I was 43 that I was introduced to who God really is.

He is the most outrageously loving, forgiving and grace-filled Father, who chose and adopted me as his precious daughter.

For me, that day, everything changed.

It was Dr Mark Stibbe who introduced me to my Dad that day. He opened my eyes to who I am and to whom I belong. I will never forget it.

At the time, Tim and I were pastoring a church in Harrogate, and we invited Mark up on a number of other occasions, as his teaching on the Father was so desperately needed and had so incredibly changed people.

When we heard the news of Mark's fall, we were just so sad. So very sad. Our most overwhelming emotion was sadness. Sadness for Mark, for his wife and especially for his children. Sadness for the ministry and for the worldwide Church.

Personally, I wanted to shake him and hug him simultaneously. Together, Tim and I prayed for those involved. Our heart was to reach out, but how? Where?

As you will hear in this amazing book, we were able to connect, to talk, to ask questions, to challenge, but most of all to love. We have never condoned but have always loved and believed that God is who he says he is, 'The God of restoration'.

You see, the more you understand your own identity, the more you believe what God says about you, and the more you understand the depth of his love and even more so his mercy and grace.

I realise that I am still on the journey of my restoration, my divine *kintsugi* if you will. Actually, we all are. We are being transformed from glory to glory.

> We can all draw close to him with the veil removed from our faces. And with no veil we all become like mirrors who brightly reflect the glory of the Lord *Jesus*. We are being transfigured into his very image as we move from one brighter level of glory to another. And this glorious transfiguration comes from the Lord, who is the Spirit.
>
> 2 Corinthians 3:18 (TPT)

I have made copious mistakes, some in private, and some more public. My Father, to whom Mark introduced me, continues to love, to forgive, to cherish, to lead, to guide and to restore me to himself. For that I am eternally grateful.

He will do the same for you.

He has done the same for Mark and the lovely Cherith. They are living testimonies of who the Father is.

They are a good news story.

They have chosen to repent, to seek council, to seek guidance. They have chosen to be accountable and they are now, so bravely, giving all that they have learnt and walked through away to you and to me in this book, to help us individually to grow and flourish in the Father's grace. They are also giving this amazing Good News to the Church.

The Church is the expression of God's heart, his Plan A for the world, and there is no Plan B.

The Church (worldwide) is God's chosen plan for the world. He tells us on many occasions that he is coming back for his Bride, his Church.

It's our responsibility to mirror, if you like, his heart for the world. Sadly, on many occasions we have not (and I readily include myself) reflected God's glory, his heart or even his word.

We have acted like the Pharisees; we have judged, we have thrown stones and we have been full of pride. My heart hurts for those we have cast out, for those we have shipwrecked and for those we have abandoned. I believe this book will help us to help ourselves and to help others.

This book has the power to heal, to bring redemption and restoration. What I believe Mark and Cherith have done in writing it is to show how they have both owned their story. Brené Brown says, "Owning our story can be hard but not nearly as difficult as spending our lives running from it. Embracing our vulnerabilities is risky but not nearly as dangerous as giving up on love and belonging and joy – the experiences that make us the most vulnerable."

Because they have owned their story and dared to share it in this book, we can grow, learn and change.

I urge you to read it with an open heart, a heart full of Jesus and a heart full of understanding.

You will laugh, cry and probably be challenged. I know I was.

What we can do once we have read it is to change our hearts, to help people change theirs and to truly be the Church that Jesus is coming back for: his Bride, ready, beautiful, full of love and compassion. A home where orphans meet their heavenly Father.

Sue Eldridge
Presence Ministries International
Co-Director, European Leaders Alliance (ELA)
Director, Alive and Kicking

P.S. What I heard from Mark all those years ago changed everything for me, to the effect that I have written and now host schools of empowerment for women called 'Alive and Kicking'. In these schools, I seek to lead women into understanding the Father, understanding their identity and walking shame-free, authentic lives, owning their stories and owning their redemption and restoration – all with the guidance of the Holy Spirit.

I wonder what you will do?

FOREWORD (2)

Jesus constantly amazed those who came to him – disciples, Pharisees and onlookers. He still does amaze, if we listen to him and follow his example.

Take the story in John 8, where a woman caught in adultery is brought to him. The Scribes – scholarly experts on the law of Moses – were religious legalists looking to catch Jesus out. They were more interested in legalism than grace. They were religious but not spiritual. Jesus reserved his harshest criticism for these Pharisees rather than the sinners he so often interacted with.

The Scribes were judgmental and legalistic; they were more interested in obeying rules than building relationships. I say 'obeying rules', even though they themselves broke or failed to fulfil the law themselves.

Jesus came to perfectly fulfil the law by completing it and instigating a new covenant of grace (Matthew 5:17). In him we have grace and mercy, but also redemption from our sins and the old nature. He was – and is – more interested in right relationships, or heart connections, than the letter of the law. This doesn't mean we need to sin to experience more of his grace. Paul warns against that in Romans 6:1. When the Pharisees brought the woman before Jesus and accused her in front of him, they wanted to entrap him. If he failed to deal with her adultery, he would have broken the law of Moses.

Interestingly, they didn't bring the man caught in adultery with her (as was required by the same law). Perhaps because their motives were less about restoring broken relationships and more about punishment to be meted out.

Jesus ignored the taunts of the Scribes and bent down and wrote with his finger in the dust. By doing this, he fulfilled Jeremiah's prophecy that those who forsake God (spiritual adultery) will be written in the dust: "...all who forsake you shall be put to shame; those who turn away from you shall be written in the earth, for they have forsaken the Lord, the fountain of living water" (Jeremiah 17:13, ESV).

Jesus responds to their angry taunts by saying, "Let's have the man who has never had a sinful desire throw the first stone at her." He went beyond the rules of the law to examine the hearts of their own relationship with the Lord. Upon hearing this, her accusers slowly left the crowd one at a time. When he was left alone with her, he asked her where her accusers were. In Verse 11 she replies, "I see no one, Lord." [Lord Yahweh! – literally her powerful testimony and revelation of who Jesus was.] Her relationship restored with him, he replies, "Neither do I put you down," or, "I don't condemn you either."

His mercy triumphed over judgment! His mercy superseded legalism. His new covenant was on display.

Then he added, "Go, and from now on, be free from a life of sin."

This last line is so important. Many miss this out, speaking about his grace but failing to notice that his grace changes our behaviour. Our relationship restored with him means we have a heart connection once again, which we do not want to break or damage through sin.

It's the kindness of God that leads us to repentance (Romans

2:4). When God put Moses in the cleft of a rock in Exodus 33:22, his glory passed by and his goodness was revealed to Moses: "Then the Lord passed by in front of him and proclaimed, 'The Lord, the Lord God, compassionate and gracious, slow to anger, and abounding in lovingkindness and truth.'" Notice that the Lord reveals his compassion, graciousness, patience and loving kindness before he reveals his truth.

Jesus demonstrated this with the woman caught in adultery. She felt his kindness, his grace, love and mercy before he spoke truth to her about sinning no more. We do well to follow Jesus' example, especially when helping to restore a friend.

In our love for Mark (and later for Cherith when we finally met her), our desire was always to accept and love them, responding in grace and mercy. By doing this we never condoned their sin of adultery, but followed the model of Jesus. He was the restorer of relationships and we are called into the same ministry of reconciliation as his. Only when people feel the kindness of our Father, demonstrated through earthly relationships, are they more likely to be open to his truth. People know when they have failed. What they need is hope that this is not the end.

All of us have fallen short of the glory of the Lord and missed the target of his goodness. But he restores. It doesn't have to be the end of the story.

As Mark so eloquently writes in this book, in Peter's restoration in John 21, Jesus takes the initiative and restores the relationship that Peter has broken.

I have always been saddened when one of our generals in the Kingdom is left to hang out and dry. Surely we should be drawing alongside them to demonstrate God's goodness, which leads to repentance? As you read this book about the personal journey of Mark and Cherith, the example of Peter in John 21, and the analogy of Japanese *kintsugi* (restoration of broken pieces), read through the eyes of God's grace and not through the eyes of judgement.

This book will challenge you.

This book must challenge our current Church culture, especially in Britain.

God always wants relationships restored.

We must too.

Tim Eldridge
Presence Ministries International

ENDORSEMENTS

I was devastated when I heard the news that my trusted friend, Mark Stibbe, had had a moral failure. He was a man I admired, and I considered it a pure joy to know and work with him (I still do). While I never could have imagined that this would happen to him and his family, here it was — inexcusable and wrong. And yet my greatest privilege in life is to represent Jesus by loving well. This means that there is only one legitimate response to this sin or, for that matter, any other: I must pursue forgiveness and restoration.

Restoring the Fallen is the beautiful but honest story of Mark and Cherith Stibbe's journey from failure into the arms of a perfect, loving Father. Simply put, this is a much-needed book that gives hope at a time when we need it most. While God never excuses sin, He consistently responds to the repentant heart with grace. And it is grace that enables us to live righteously. I pray that this wonderful book would serve as a template for years to come, enabling us to stop being the only army on the earth who shoots their wounded. Instead, we must love these dear ones back into health.

The Stibbes' story is brilliantly illustrated in the Japanese art called *kintsugi*, where a broken vessel is made even more beautiful than before it was broken. This is a profound illustration of grace. It provides us with a picture that should inspire every believer to look for opportunities to seek for restoration. Believe it or not, we need the broken restored. Plus, we are in great need of the perspective of love and grace that these healed ones could bring into our lives. It would make us much more complete. This timely message must be embraced for us to really see the heart of the Father released into the earth.

Bill Johnson
Senior Pastor of Bethel Church, Redding, California

I'm fairly certain most of us will have heard of individuals who have had similar experiences to Mark and Cherith, some even amongst their close friends. However, I am not aware of any couples who have been brave enough to go to print and share in technicolour honesty their personal journey in the way this book does.

I'm sure the Prodigal was eternally grateful to be met by the Father and not the Elder Brother. No wonder Paul says we need more fathers. This heart-revealing book records the journey back to the Father and I fully recommend both the book and the authors to you.

David Campbell
Regional Leader, Metropolitan East and
West Regions, Elim Pentecostal Church

Why did we ever think that living together with broken, imperfect people was going to be anything less than messy? The question we now must ask is: "How do we love people through their mess?" To answer this, Mark and Cherith have produced a fantastic book which should challenge you to your core. The ministry of *Restoring the Fallen* is going to be a future hallmark of a glorious Church.

Years ago, after major hurts and wounds, I heard Mark Stibbe teach a powerful message of healing and restoration and it changed my life. A few years ago, it was a privilege to make space for this fallen giant and give him a platform in our house. And now, today, I count it an absolute honour to commend Mark and Cherith and their brand new book to you.

Adam Graves
Senior Leader, FreshFire Church, Manchester
Director, The Restoration Centre

The song lines, "beauty for brokenness, hope for despair" kept running through my mind as I read this book in one sitting.

That is the heart message of this book, earthed in the reality of Mark and Cherith's experience.

This story could easily be any of ours, because any of us can fall.

Any of us!

The message of this book is that restoration and hope can be ours as well, in the hands of the heavenly Potter.

Read it and weep!

Lynne
Association of Christian Counsellors
(Mark's Counsellor, 2013-2015)

This book helps to reflect the Father's heart of love to us all. As the battle rages for biblical principles and godly living, *Restoring the Fallen* is a rallying cry to the Church to tend to rather than shoot its wounded.

Mark and Cherith's journey is a demonstration of all parts of the army of God working together to restore two of God's masterpieces.

We trust that their honesty and openness will bring new hope and help to the fallen, who sadly remain untreated in the army of God.

Indeed, may the Stibbes' testimony of repentance and restoration lead to many others being given support, so they can return with them to the front lines once more.

Hugh and Ginny Cryer
Founders of Culture Changers
culture-changers.org

As a member of Mark's ministry team at *The Father's House Trust*, when he left Watford I felt immense sorrow that I may not see again the one person who had brought so much understanding to my intimate walk with my heavenly Father. However, healing between us came very rapidly as Mark made himself totally transparent and accountable to those who had believed in him as a person and as a minister.

When he and Cherith decided that it was the right path to separate in March 2013, Mark felt a great sense of concern for who was really there for Cherith. Although I didn't know Cherith very well, I felt that it was important to get to know her.

We met at the National Gallery in London and after a brief look at the treasures, I found the greatest treasure of all that day in Cherith (over a four-hour lunch eating kedgeree!).

From that moment on I have cherished Cherith and her gentleness, thoughtfulness, kindness, wit and warmth.

Cherith has much to say of great gravitas, beauty and wisdom, and I am delighted that in absolute truth Mark and Cherith have chosen to share their 'journey home' with the world.

I pray you will be as blessed as I have been to walk with them through their continuing journey in giving glory to the incredible Father of all kindness, compassion and restoration, and in giving thanks for those who seek his likeness.

Juliette
Christian Counsellor

The Scriptures teach that, "If a man be overtaken in a fault, ye which are spiritual, restore such a one in the spirit of meekness; considering thyself, least thou also be tempted."

Unfortunately, the Church has had a great deal of difficulty walking in this truth. Instead of considering ourselves and restoring gently, we have been guilty of judging, condemning and throwing away.

As I have had the privilege of walking along this journey with Mark and Cherith, the Holy Spirit has taught me how to love without judgement, seek to understand with meekness, and love without condition. These qualities of the Kingdom are what Mark and Cherith share so beautifully and bravely through their own personal story and the story of Jesus and Peter.

I believe this book is a blueprint for what we need to learn in the Body of Christ: that our brokenness is an incredible opportunity for the Master to goldenly glue us back together for a greater destiny.

Restoring The Fallen is a must-read for those of us who may have fallen, and those of us who need to bring restoration to our beloved brothers and sisters.

Theresa Goode
Co-Founder and Senior Pastor of New Dimension
Apostolic Centre, Rhode Island, USA

I was once asked by a young pastor what criteria I would use to decide whether to invite a man to minister who had a history of a moral fall. My reply was that if it was my church or event, then my decision would be based on whether I had witnessed godly sorrow and repentance. Once this condition had been met, I would have no hesitation.

It was my privilege to spend time with Mark in private and to observe his repentance first hand. It was this that enabled me to introduce him to a conference audience and now to endorse his book.

As I read the manuscript I was drawn to the references to the Japanese art of *kintsugi*, in which the value of a bowl that has been beautifully and skilfully repaired is greater than the original. Some years ago, I spent time with an elderly prophet whose words have stuck with me: "Show me the scar and I will show you the man." Mark is showing us the man, 'scars and all'. This requires vulnerability and courage.

One of the great needs in the Church today is for us to truly learn and demonstrate how to restore the fallen, especially leaders. Of course, my great desire is that we learn how to prevent such falls, but the Gospel of Jesus

Christ carries the invitation to repent and the promise of restoration. *Restoring the Fallen* showcases this Gospel, the Gospel of the Kingdom, for which our Redeemer laid down his life.

Paul Manwaring
Senior Leadership Team,
Bethel Church, Redding, California
Author and International Speaker

A LETTER FROM MARK & CHERITH

Dear Readers,

We want you to know, right at the outset, that we are deeply sorry for all the pain we have caused through our actions seven years ago. We hurt people who mean the world to us, and while we have sought to say sorry whenever God has opened the door, we may have not had the opportunity to say sorry to everyone. If you are one of those, know that we are not glib about the suffering we have inflicted. The thought of it has always filled us with sorrow. We are truly sorry. Please forgive us.

Also, we are very aware that some of the pain we have caused has been because our actions have reminded you of past wounds, past desertions, past rejections. We are so sorry if that's the case for you. There may be moments when you read, even perhaps before you read, when you feel rage towards us for what we have done, because our story reminds you in some way of what others have done to you in the past.

We don't want to add to the pain, but both of us would offer this one thought: if you can release this pain to the Father, especially the sense of disappointment and abandonment, then we believe that this book could profoundly help you on your journey of healing and freedom.

While no two stories are the same, our loving Father remains the same yesterday, today and forever. And he is unrelentingly loving towards those who have failed and those who have been hurt by that failure, wooing us all into a place where we can exchange our sorrow into joy, our mourning into dancing.

Our Father is too kind to leave the prodigals in the 'far country', and too compassionate to neglect those hurt by their actions.

Our prayer is that our story, and the truths we have learned on the way, will encourage you and speak to you, so that we can all enjoy the glorious freedom of the children of God.

When our hearts are ready, may we all come home to the Love of all loves.

Mark and Cherith

The world breaks everyone, and afterward many
are strong at the broken places.[i]

Ernest Hemingway
Novelist

1

IT'S NOT ALL OVER

At the beginning of September 2012, I was enjoying a good income and widespread influence as a Christian speaker. I was regularly preaching and lecturing on church and non-church stages all over the world, sometimes to 5,000 people at a time. I was appearing on radio and TV shows and writing for magazines and newspapers. I was the author of over thirty books, as well as the leader of a charity I had founded called *The Father's House Trust*.

You could say I had everything, at least on the surface; a marriage that seemed to be strong and four healthy children.

By the end of that same month, like so many other prominent preachers before and after me, I had fallen morally in a way that hurt people near and far.

And in an instant, I lost it all.

It was the darkest and most shameful moment of my life.

During the months that followed, I wrestled with my conscience in the 'far country'. The 'far country' is where the prodigal son found himself when he rebelled against his father's love. In the famous parable in Luke 15, this boy – the younger son – loses his fortune and ends up wallowing in a pigpen during a famine. There he comes to his senses and decides to return to his father, which is exactly what I did in March 2013.

After seven months of languishing in rebellious isolation, I laid everything down and said sorry to my Father in heaven, and subsequently to those that I cared about most and had hurt most deeply. That was an extremely hard thing to do. It took every last vestige of courage in my despondent heart.

As I started to rebuild my life, one thing became abundantly and quickly clear to me: the Church at large has little idea how to restore fallen and fractured people. Worse still, few people seemed to have the appetite for it.

In the circles I had moved in before the fall, people had talked a lot about renewal, revival and even reformation, but there was one 'R' missing – *restoration*. I found it so hard to find people who shared the Father's longing to see his children restored after they have fallen. It seemed to me then, and it seems to me now, that this is a taboo subject. We'd much rather not admit that such failures happen at all. If we do, we often not only fail to ask the tough questions about *why* these falls occur, but we don't ask *how* we are going to pick people up after they have fallen.

This book is an attempt to address this deficit; it is my story, yes, but it is also a strategy. A strategy that one day, I found in a beautiful passage in the Gospel of John, and in a particularly compelling ceramic artform from the unfamiliar world of Japanese pottery.

Kintsugi.

Golden Joinery

I came across the Japanese idea of *kintsugi* in 2014, and subsequently mentioned it in my book *Home at Last*.

Kintsugi is a combination of two Japanese words: *kin*, meaning 'gold', and *tsugi*, meaning 'joinery'. *Kintsugi* is literally 'golden joinery'. It is the Japanese art of taking hold of broken pieces of pottery and putting them back together.

Kintsugi involves using a lacquer that acts as a glue, with gold dust added to the mix. This lacquer binds all the fragments together and causes the repaired pot to display its cracks in bright gold.

When I heard about *kintsugi*, it felt like an epiphany.

On the surface, *kintsugi* is practical and physical. It involves hands-on techniques designed to restore material objects. But it is more than that. Kintsugi is firmly rooted in a spiritual philosophy known as *wabi-sabi*. *Wabi-sabi* teaches that we must renounce our insatiable appetite for perfection in art and life and learn instead to appreciate that beauty can best be found and seen in imperfect things.

When a priceless vase is broken, it is not to be thrown away. Nothing is to be wasted. The fragments must be picked up, their edges pasted with golden lacquer, and then glued back together. Then, when the restoration is complete, the repaired pot, with its vivid veins of gold, is to be regarded as more beautiful and more valuable than the original.

That is a startling picture of restoration! And it is one that immediately challenges our Western ways of thinking. Addicted as we are to consumerism, we see broken things as instantly disposable. When something is broken, our reflex is not to restore it but to replace it. We throw the pieces away in our ever-bulging bins and we head off to the nearest store to buy a replacement.

And here's the worrying thing: We don't just do this to *things*. We do it to *human beings,* too. In this regard, we show not only how impoverished our values are in comparison with *kintsugi*, we also show how far away we are from the values of the Kingdom of heaven. In our Father's Kingdom, people are not commodities either. They are his precious children.

In the Father's hands, broken people are restored when they fall.

And they shine more brightly for it.

The Heavenly Potter

Prior to my fall, I wrote many books on the subject of the Father's love and our calling to be his adopted children. It was my life's message. In fact, my entire speaking and writing career can be summed up in a quotation from my favourite Christian author, Father Brennan Manning. He once remarked that the central revelation of Jesus Christ in the New Testament is that God is our *Abba*, our Daddy. I agree.

This was the theme of my writing. God is the Daddy we've all been waiting for, the greatest Papa in the universe, and he's waiting, like the father of the prodigal son, for all of us to find our heart's true home in his intimate, healing embrace.

That said, in everything I ever wrote or preached, I never commented on one particular Old Testament text where God is specifically called 'Father'. I am referring to Isaiah 64:8, which, for me, is now one of the most important verses in the Bible:

Yet you, Lord, are our Father.
We are the clay; you are the Potter.
We are all the work of your hands.

Two things are said about God here.

First of all, he is our Father. We are his children, and he is the most affectionate, compassionate, intimate Dad you could ever imagine.

Secondly, this Father is also a divine Potter. He shapes his children over time into vessels that he can display for his glory.

In light of this revelation, this is what I want to say, right at the outset of this book. Our heavenly Father is the ultimate source of *kintsugi*. Yes, the ideas may derive from Zen spirituality, but I believe the principle behind it comes directly from the Father heart of God. *Abba* Father, after all, doesn't despise broken people; he specialises in putting us back together again. When we fall, he gathers up the pieces of our lives and works skilfully to mend us.

For a physical pot, being broken is not the end of the story. And it is not the end of the story for us either. In the Kingdom of heaven, we are all repaired when we fall, if we offer ourselves to the divine Potter.

And once restored, we are regarded as more beautiful and valuable than we were before, because the gold of God's glory shines through every imperfection, bringing out the divine brilliance in our human brokenness.

As the Apostle Paul said, "We have this treasure in jars of clay to show that this all-surpassing power is from God and not from us" (2 Corinthians 4:6-7). Without the cracks, no one would see the gold!

After the Fall

All this brings me to a chapter of the Bible where we see 'heaven's blueprint for restoration'. I am referring to John 21, a chapter devoted almost entirely to Jesus' restoration of Simon Peter. If ever there was a Bible passage that highlighted the point that being broken is not the end of the story, it's John 21.

Think about it for a moment. In John 20, we see the risen Jesus appearing to his disciples, beginning with Mary Magdalene.

The Lord is risen. The disciples are overjoyed. What a powerful conclusion to the story!

To confirm the point, here are the final words of John 20:

> Jesus performed many other signs in the presence of his disciples, which are not recorded in this book. But these are written that you may believe that Jesus is the Messiah, the Son of God, and that by believing you may have life in his name.

Just when we thought it was finished, John adds another chapter.

Why?

Think back to John 18-19, the story of Jesus' arrest, trials, torture and execution. This story, known as the passion narrative, is really two stories. The first is about our hero, Jesus. The second is about Peter, nicknamed 'Rocky' – a word denoting steadfastness, immovability, strength, and toughness. Except that, ironically, Peter doesn't show any of these qualities when he is under pressure. In the courtyard of the High Priest Annas, Peter stands by the fire as Jesus is taken off to be interrogated by the religious leaders. As Jesus is questioned inside the house, Peter is questioned outside by a servant girl. She asks him three times if he's one of Jesus' disciples. Peter replies, "I am not!"

"I am not?"

Look at the irony here. In a Gospel where Jesus frequently declares, "I Am", Peter says, "I am not!" In a Gospel where Jesus calls himself "the Light of the World", Peter warms himself by a man-made fire, declaring without words where he stands.

Jesus had prophesied that Peter would deny him three times.

Now all that has come true.

Peter has fallen.

No wonder John adds another chapter after what sounds like a terrific ending.

There is one storyline yet to be finished. There is one question still left hanging. What about Simon Peter? What happened after the fall?

The Artist at Work

John 21 provides the answer. Here we see the risen Jesus standing early one morning by the Sea of Galilee. Peter has invited six other disciples and friends to go out fishing with him. They have caught nothing. Jesus shouts to them, telling them where they need to drop the nets. Now they catch a huge haul of fish.

At this point the beloved disciple recognises Jesus.

"It's the Lord!" he cries.

Peter reacts instantly and irrationally. He puts on his clothes, dives into the sea, and swims the short distance to the shore where he finds Jesus sitting by a fire, preparing breakfast.

What follows is one of the most moving scenes in the entire Bible.

Once the disciples have had their fill of barbequed fish and toasted bread, Jesus focuses on Peter. He asks him three questions about the extent of his love for him. Three times Peter answers, the third time with obvious anguish.

This is a powerful process.

In fact, it is divine *kintsugi*.

Yes, Peter has fallen badly. He has failed to make his stand when questioned by a mere servant girl. Three times he has denied being Jesus' disciple. After the third time, the cock crowed, just as Jesus foretold. By any standards, this is disloyalty. However understandable, Peter has been cowardly. Destined to be a leader in the earliest Church, he has buckled under pressure. He has fallen.

But this is not the end of Peter's story, any more than it is the end of ours, if we too have fallen. Jesus is the Father's *kintsugi* master, and Peter is a broken pot. Watch the master at work in John 21 as he puts the pieces back together again, glues the fragments into a new whole, all with the golden and glorious power of the Father's healing power.

Watch and wonder! This is amazing grace indeed! Now the Gospel of John can end. And so it does. Even more beautifully than in the closing verses of John 20. Listen to John's resounding flourish:

> Jesus did many other things as well. If every one of them were written down, I suppose that even the whole world would not have room for the books that would be written.

Now that's what I call an ending!

It's Not the End

In one of the most famous moments of sport's commentary, perhaps the most famous, Kenneth Wolstenholme described the closing moments of England's victory over West Germany in the FIFA 1966 World Cup Final.

English spectators were running onto the Wembley pitch to celebrate a 3-2 triumph.

Except that the final whistle had not been blown by the referee.

And England player Geoff Hurst was bearing down unerringly on the West German goal, the ball at his feet.

The commentator sees the invading crowd and remarks that there are people on the pitch.

"They think it's all over!" he cries, pointing to the intruders.

As he finishes that sentence, Hurst belts the ball into the West German net, making the score 4-2.

Wolstenholme shouts, in a now much-quoted phrase, "It is now!"

When a person falls, many people in the Church, unaware of heaven's blueprint for restoration, think it's all over. If they perceive from a distance that the person remains unrepentant (according to their standards), they cry, "It is now!"

But this is a theological mistake born of judgmentalism, devoid of kindness, and bloated with that, oh-so-deadly, sin of pride.

In short, it is religion-based, not Kingdom-based thinking.

In the Kingdom of heaven, as soon as a fallen person submits to the restorative love of the Father, the game is no longer over. The story is no longer finished. Something beautiful and victorious is in play, so much so that in the future, the person will not be defined by their failure, but rather by the courageous way in which they turned their mess into a message.

From Dad's Perspective

For those who think this is cheap or even hyper grace, remember this: the Bible is full of heroes who fell but who got up again, who dusted themselves down and continued to run the race of faith.

Think of Adam and Eve, the archetypal and primal fallen heroes, by whom we are all represented, to whom we are all related, and from whom we are all recipients of a fallen sin nature. They fell, repented, received forgiveness, got up again, and led godly and productive lives.

Moses murdered a man in cold blood, but was sent to the desert for a period of restoration before being commissioned to lead God's people out of Egypt.

David, having seen Bathsheba bathing, had her husband killed and committed adultery with her. He repented, received forgiveness, and lived a godly life with Bathsheba from that time on.

And what's even more startling is the fact that none of these heroes is defined by their failure, at least in heaven.

Take David, for example. Long after he is dead and buried, one thousand years after to be precise, the Apostle Paul summed his life up as follows: "When David had served God's purpose in his own generation, he fell asleep" (Acts 13:32). No mention of David's crime of murder or sin of adultery.

A few years before, Jesus had been happy to be known as "the son of David". He never objected on the grounds that David had broken two of the Commandments. He wasn't angry about being associated with David, or about being related to him either.

And when Matthew came to write the genealogy of Jesus, he included Bathsheba. Why? Because heaven is not ashamed of these fallen men and women. They repented, were restored, and lived godly and fruitful lives – in David and Bathsheba's case, as a married couple.

Heaven Vs Religion

I remember how startled I was when I was writing a book on the Passion Bible Translation of The Book of Proverbs. I had the honour of writing the devotional commentaries for both The Book of Proverbs and The Book of Psalms. As I was nearing the end, I came across this passage at the beginning of Proverbs 31:

These are the inspired words my mother taught me. "Listen, my dear son, son of my womb. You are the answer to my prayers, my son. So keep yourself sexually pure ... you are to be a king who speaks up on behalf of the disenfranchised and pleads for the legal rights of the defenceless and those who are dying. Be a righteous king, judging on behalf of the poor and interceding for those most in need."

Who is speaking here?
King Solomon.
Who is he quoting?
His mother.
Who was his mother?
Bathsheba!
That's stunning!
Bathsheba wasn't finished when she fell. As David's wife, she went on to be a woman of God in her own right. She became a righteous wife to David and a righteous mother to Solomon. She was not disqualified. She wasn't defined by her failure. She rose up again and fought on for God's values here on earth; values to do with personal holiness and social justice. Her voice was not silenced by religion. It was released by heaven.

And so it will be for you and me, if we allow ourselves to be restored, and if the Christians who surround us reflect the kindness of heaven rather than the sternness of religion.

A Terrible Penalty

In the FIFA European Championships in 1996, England were once again facing Germany. This time it was the semi-finals. If they won, they'd be in the final, with an excellent chance of winning a major cup for the first time since 1966. The match went to penalties.

A defender walked up to the goal to take the decisive penalty.

His name?

Gareth Southgate.

He missed the penalty, and England were eliminated from the tournament.

Today, Southgate is the manager of the England team. At the time of writing, he has taken his players to the semi-finals of FIFA's 2018 World Cup. A remarkable achievement for such a young squad.

Furthermore, he coached his players to win a penalty shootout against Colombia in a crucial knockout game.

Gareth Southgate said this: "I've learnt a million things from the day I missed a penalty … the biggest being that when something goes wrong in your life, it doesn't finish you."[ii]

That is *kintsugi*.

If you've fallen and are fractured, if you've experienced failure and despair, it's not the end of the story.

Religious people may say, "It's all over."

But in the master's hands, your story is about to begin again. Just as Peter's did.

Cherith Adds

I thought it was all over. The biggest mistake I made after my fall was believing that my heavenly Father no longer cared, no longer loved me, was ashamed of me. This was the reaction of many of my Christian friends and, as we're being honest, if it had been someone else's fall it would probably have been my reaction too. At the end of the day, what I had done was a choice and it was *my choice*. When I had my moral fall, I was already a Christian. Did I really deserve another chance?

Mark talks about 'languishing in rebellious isolation'. That is exactly how I felt. I reached a stage where I felt safer in the pigpen than I did in Church. When I finally plucked up the courage to crawl out of the pigpen, my heavenly Daddy was there.

And he wasn't standing with his arms crossed, looking down on me with condemnation.

He was right there with me, beckoning me into his arms. He wooed me into repentance with a love that I knew I didn't deserve.

I didn't particularly want to write this book. It's raw and it's vulnerable and frankly, it's none of your business!

Except that it is.

It may be your business because you are broken, you've messed up, or you're on the edge of doing something you'll live to regret.

It may be your business because you have friends or family members who have made mistakes, have sinned, or are living a lifestyle you don't agree with.

I have been on both sides of this fence and it's much easier looking into the pigpen than it is looking out from it.

This is part of my story, but it's not who I am. It has taken me a long time to realise that and some days, I have to fight to keep believing it.

My prayer is that our story offers some hope to those who have given up on themselves and a challenge to those who have given up on others.

When given the choice between being right or being kind, choose kind.[iii]

R J Palacio
Author

2

KINTSUGI, THE JESUS WAY

One of the things I learned after my fall was the difference between those I thought were my friends, and those who really were my friends. What I quickly saw was that there were many people who had loved my 'ministry', but there were fewer people who had loved *me*. Their friendship was not related to my reputation. Whether I was standing under the spotlights being applauded, or languishing in hiddenness feeling ashamed, they simply loved Mark.

I will never stop being grateful for their extraordinary kindness.

Among those friends were Dave and Mandy, leaders in the Elim Pentecostal Church of Great Britain. Dave made it very clear to me that what I had done was wrong. He owed it to me to tell me the truth and he was faithful to God in doing that, and in emphasising that there were consequences to my actions that I was going to have to live with for a long time.

The way Dave and Mandy went about that was fair and firm as well as kind and compassionate. It was a model of how to behave towards the fallen, filled as it was with 'grace and truth'. As it says in Proverbs 27:6, "faithful are the wounds of a friend."

Dave and Mandy walked with me through those early days, weeks and months, when it cost them to be my friends, when they had to take some hits to even be associated with me. But as I began to work my way through the process of returning to the Father, Dave said something that injected a ray of hope into my heart. I was in particular need of encouragement that day, and I suspect my friend saw it.

"Mark, it's not the end of the book," he said. "It's simply the end of a chapter."

What a great thing to say to someone who's an author!

That single sentence, which Dave repeated several times over the following months when I needed it, gave me a glimpse of the Father's kindness. Like a *kintsugi* master, God had not finished with me. In fact, he was only just beginning. He was picking up the pieces, preparing the glue, and getting ready to pour the gold of his healing into the cracks in my heart.

A Broken Teacup

There's a lovely story behind the origins of *kintsugi*. It all began in the fifteenth century when the eighth shogun of the Muromachi period broke one of his favourite teacups. The story goes that Ashiga Yoshimasa dropped the cup and was devastated. He sent it to China for repairs but when the object was returned, he was horrified to find that the restorers had simply stitched the cracks back together with tiny metal braces. The cup now looked uglier than it had when it was smashed on the floor.

Determined not to throw the cup away, the shogun asked the ceramic artists in his circle to come up with a way of repairing it. The method they invented has stood the test of time. It is, like all the best art, profound in its simplicity. Here is their process of restoration:

Stage 1: They began by studying the fragments of the cup, placing them in the right positions in preparation for the gluing process.

Stage 2: They mixed the ingredients needed for the glue, forming an adhesive lacquer out of water, flour, gold dust and the sap of a local plant.

Stage 3: Once the lacquer was ready, they applied it to the cracks, gluing the cup back together again, keeping everything in place with bands.

Stage 4: The repaired teacup was left to cure in a warm, wet environment – on a plate with water in a small, *muro* box near a heat source.

Stage 5: After anytime between a week and a month, the cup was taken from the box and the excess lacquer delicately removed.

When the cup was brought before the shogun, he loved what he saw.

He put the teacup in a visible place, saying that the golden scars should always be on display, and that the damage should never be disguised. In doing so, he gave voice to his belief that there was great beauty in his new and imperfect teacup; a beauty greater than he had ever seen when the cup was perfect.

So, the art of *kintsugi* was born and the *kintsugi* ritual of restoration had been set in stone.

The brilliant *kintsugi* masters, inspired by their Zen philosophy of wasting nothing, had given new life to the teacup, and the shogun was delighted.

Jesus, the Restorer

Let's return to the story of Jesus' restoration of Simon Peter. We know already from John's Gospel that every word and action of Jesus is a revelation of the Father. When Philip had said to Jesus, "Show us the Father," Jesus simply replied, "He who has seen me has seen the Father." In other words (paraphrased), "Philip, don't you get it? My words are the Father's words. My deeds are the Father's deeds" (John 14:8-9).

When Jesus meets with Simon Peter in John 21, what we are witnessing is the Father's process of restoration. It is our heavenly Dad at work, putting the broken pieces of Peter's life back together. This is divine *kintsugi*, because God is not only our Father, he is also our Potter.

For the rest of this book, we are going to study, admire and learn from every stage of this divine *kintsugi*. As we begin to do that, I want to focus on one thing that forms the basis of it all, and that is Jesus' exceptional kindness. Nothing would ever have happened without this. It is the single most important factor in establishing the very possibility of restoration. Without it, Peter would very likely have gone back to his former life of fishing and remained there, a broken man full of shame. But because of Jesus' divine kindness, Peter was restored. Like a *kintsugi* vase, he was given new life. His scars were now on display, but these cracks made him more precious, not just to God but to us. Why? Because they not only reveal the beauty of God's healing power, they are also what makes Peter *relatable* as a model for every fallen, imperfect, fractured human being.

And that, if we are truly honest, is every single one of us.

So, we begin with the foundation of restoration – the Father's kindness. As Saint Paul says, "it is the kindness of God that leads to repentance" (Romans 2:4). It is the fact that God comes to us not with stern looks and angry words, but with eyes of love and words of affirmation, that we turn away from our rebellion and begin the journey home. However much this may offend those of a religious sensibility, the truth is that the Father's kindness is not confined to the Father's house. It reaches into the 'far country', even into the pigpen, because he knows full well that it is not his sternness that will draw us home, but his kindness. This is one of his ways. *Kintsugi*, in God's hands, is *kindsugi*.

Just as the devoted *kintsugi* master does not rage against the broken pot, but looks lovingly on every fractured piece determined to give it a new lease of life, so our Father does not rail against us when we fail or fall. He is already gazing upon our brokenness, planning how to bring something infinitely more beautiful and valuable out of our mess.

This is what we see in John 21. Jesus could have written Peter off and replaced him, but Jesus is not a Messiah who regards his followers as disposable commodities. He is our perfect older Brother who looks upon us with extreme love. He is better than the best friend, greater than the greatest older brother. As the Book of Proverbs says, "there is a friend who sticks closer than a brother." His name is Jesus.

The Power of Kindness

For many years, my father was headteacher at a school in Norwich, Norfolk (UK). One summer, at the end-of-year gathering for the entire school, the great comic genius Stephen Fry was the guest speaker. There were many gems in his address, but the most memorable moment came when he started to extol the virtue of kindness. He told all the schoolchildren, teachers and parents that he had met many of the world's most celebrated people during his life but he only remembered few of them in his heart. The ones whose memories he held dear were not the most talented, nor the wealthiest. They were the ones who were *kind*.

What, then, do we mean by 'kindness'? Joseph Joubert defines it as "loving people more than they deserve". This is exactly what we see in Jesus. Jesus appears on the shores of Galilee for just one man: Simon Peter. He takes time to make breakfast for just one purpose: to restore Simon Peter. He speaks exclusively to Peter for one simple reason: he sees the beauty even in Peter's brokenness, the miracle in Peter's mess. This is divine kindness; he loves Peter more than he deserves.

It is this kindness, along with the smell of fried fish and burning coals, that establishes the atmosphere in which lasting and profound restoration can happen. Far from judging Peter, far from castigating him, Jesus accepts him, sits with him, eats with him, encourages him and heals him.

How different this is from religion, where people are either outright judgmental, or they exhibit a kind of fake kindness, a *faux* pity, that acts as a mask for their true purpose, which is not compassion but condemnation. No, Jesus reveals the values of heaven in the way he treats Peter. He sees the priceless in the worthless and chooses to focus on the priceless.

Authentically Loving

There is a danger, of course, in all this talk of kindness, especially in the context of restoration. When anyone starts emphasising kindness, some earnest Pharisee somewhere pipes up that we are being 'soft on sin'. The assumption here is that being kind means being morally lax. But this is wrong. Nowhere does Jesus say he approves of what Peter has done in denying him three times. Nor does his kindness mean that Jesus is advocating that now anything goes in Peter's life. Kindness does not mean a loss of moral sensitivity, nor permission to sin in order to experience grace. If it did, that would make Jesus less than the perfect Messiah. No, kindness means being authentically loving to the fallen. So loving, in fact, that restoration is irresistible.

This is imperative today, as so many fallen people are put off going through the restoration process because they believe that they are not safe in the hands of those seeking to help them. Their comforters may talk a good game, but fallen, fractured people do not trust them, and I can understand why.

There are a couple of warning signs to watch out for if you have fallen.

If a person comes up to you and says, "What I'm about to say, I'm going to say in love," run for the hills. In my life, when someone has used the phrase 'in love', it has been followed by something that is often judgmental and controlling. This is not just my story but the story of many people I've spoken to in recent years.

If someone says, "I'm saying this to you because I love you," followed by, "You know I love you, don't you?" – take cover! If they have to use the phrase "because I love you", trust me, they don't. Anyone who's a true friend will not have to *tell* you that they love you. You will know it from who they are towards you and what they do for you in your season of trouble.

Remember, when Jesus engaged in the restoration process, he didn't have to say, "Now Peter, what I'm about to say is in love." Peter knew that everything Jesus said was 'in love'. Every one of his words was an earthly rendition of the Father's heavenly voice; a voice that is always uttered with the intonation of love. Jesus had loved Peter authentically since the beginning.

Likewise, Jesus didn't have to say to Peter, "You know I love you, don't you?" The evidence was already overwhelming. Jesus had just died on the Cross. He had just been to hell and back for Peter. As Jesus himself said, "Greater love has no man than this, that he lay down his life for his friends" (John 15:13).

Jesus didn't need to resort to religious platitudes or empty jargon to tell Peter how much he loved him. As we will see later, it was Peter who needed to tell Jesus how much he loved him, which is why three times Jesus asks Peter, "Do you love me?" Peter's confession that he really did love Jesus was only made possible because Jesus was so extraordinarily kind. He could have been so stern and critical with Peter. But he chose to be gentle and tender. Why? Because kindness was and is the default setting of his character.

So then, don't be superficial and simple-minded. Being kind does not mean being tolerant of wrongdoing. It means being authentically loving to those who have fallen. This love, when it is real, is the single most helpful factor in drawing a person back into the arms of the Father.

Acceptance, not Approval

This brings me back to my dear friends, Dave and Mandy. About ten years ago, I popped into a church not far from where I lived. The meeting had already begun. Trying to find a seat, I bumped into Dave, who was standing by a bookstall, looking downcast. This surprised me. Dave is renowned for being a joy-bringer.

I walked up to my friend and gave him a hug, whereupon he poured out his heart. He shared with me then what he has since spoken of publicly in many places all over the world, of his discovery that day that his unmarried daughter Amy was pregnant. I had never seen Dave so upset before then, nor have I since.

Later, Dave told me what he had said to Amy. He had not in any way attempted to minimise or trivialise what Amy had done. He talked to her about the consequences in her life, and the consequences to them as a family. But in all of this he stressed to her one thing: that he was and would always be her father, that he would support her through all the trials ahead, and that his love, and Mandy's, was unconditional.

Today, whenever I hear Dave tell this story, I am always deeply moved, not only because I have always had a great affection for Amy, but also because Dave speaks as a father, and his love for his daughter gives us a glimpse of our heavenly Father, who is also unconditionally loving, both in our success and our failure.

But here's the point: this kindness is not to be understood as approval for things that are wrong. That is to confuse acceptance with approval, and the two are not the same. As Dave said to Amy, "There is a difference between acceptance and approval. I may not approve of what you have done, but I do accept you completely and unconditionally."

This is the kind of attitude that makes divine *kintsugi* possible. When we fall, as we try to get up again, we need to feel safe with the people around us. We need to know that those people accept us unconditionally, even if they cannot and should not approve of our actions. We need to see Jesus in them; the Jesus that met with Peter by the sea. Peter knew that his Master's love for him as a person didn't mean approval of his rebellion.

Kindness is everything, but kindness does not mean condoning sin. It means gently helping people who have fallen to their feet again. It means not writing them off, not disposing of them, not replacing them. It means releasing the redemptive arc in the story of their brokenness.

And redemption is the Father's specialty. When Amy's child was born, she called her Neveah, which is 'heaven' spelt backwards, and Neveah is a princess in the Kingdom of heaven! I know this because I had the immense honour of being invited by Amy to bless Neveah in a church dedication service, and we have kept in touch ever since.

So, never forget: ugly beginnings can lead to beautiful outcomes when the risen Jesus comes strolling along your beach with kindness in his eyes.

A Mother's Words

Finally, I want to tell you about something that my mother said. It was about six weeks after my fall. My brother and I were in touch but I hadn't contacted my mother. I wasn't sure what she would say.

In the end, I caved in to my brother's pleas and rang Mum one Sunday night.

"Ah, thank goodness," she said in a faltering voice. "I've been so worried about you, Mark. I'm not cross with you so please don't avoid speaking to me or visiting me. I just wanted to know that you're all right, and I wanted to tell you that I love you."

My family was not one for saying "I love you". We were rather more detached emotionally, subscribers to the 'stiff upper lip' philosophy of the British boarding school system. So, when I heard Mum say "I love you", I was relieved that she wasn't angry with me, but I was also deeply touched that she was being so demonstrative in her affection for me.

Just before the conversation ended, she said something unexpected: "Mark, never forget, you are a much treasured son." And with that, she said goodbye.

It was a good while before I could speak.

Through my mother's words, I heard my heavenly Father.

You are still my beloved son, and I love and treasure you.

That, for me, was a turning point.

From that moment, I knew it was only a matter of time before I started coming home to my Father.

This was kindness in the 'far country'.

This was my family reaching out to me.

And there's a *big* lesson here.

The Church will never collaborate in divine *kintsugi* until we all learn to be a family; a safe place for everyone. Only when we start being kind to one another, as Jesus was with Peter, will we be able to say with the hymn writer, that we are all truly "ransomed, healed, restored, forgiven". Remember what Teresa of Avila once said: "God is even kinder than you think."[iv]

Isn't it time that we showed each other undeserved love?

Isn't it time we cooked breakfast for each other, and sat on the sand together, showing what it means to be authentically loving?

This is *kintsugi* indeed.

The Jesus way.

Cherith Adds

I will never forget meeting Dave and Mandy for the first time. Just a few days before, one of my dearest friends had phoned me to say she would only be prepared to speak to me again if I repented and changed my ways. This is exactly what I expected from Dave and Mandy. I had messed up. These people had never met me before. Mark assured me that they loved him, but somehow that made it worse. Would they blame me for leading him astray too? Yet, amidst this fear, there was something pulling me towards them. Something inside me knew it was important for me to face up to it all, no matter how painful.

I remember walking into their home, palms sweaty, heart racing, stomach churning.

Dave came to greet us.

Here we go, I thought.

We spent the next couple of hours chatting to them. Not once did either of them say they condoned what we had done, and not once did they say they condemned us. My defences came crashing down in the atmosphere of unconditional love.

This was the first time I felt guilty for what I had done and not ashamed of who I was. You see, my friend was right; I did need to repent, but it was never going to happen in a place where I didn't feel safe. Shame had kept me in the pigpen.

A few months later, I was living on my own, having started my journey towards repentance. One evening after work, I phoned my Aunt Lou. Aunt Lou was the 90-year-old grand matriarch in our family. Everyone adored her. From the moment I fell to the moment I got back on my feet, she never once interrogated me, judged me, or made me feel like she loved me any less. Perhaps it was a case of 'don't mention the war', but whatever the reason, I appreciated it!

Now, for the first time since my fall, I felt brave enough to talk to her. To apologise for hurting her and letting her down. I will never forget what she said:

"I was there the day you were born and I'm here for you now."

That's all she said about it and that's all she ever said about it. And it's all I needed.

Never underestimate the power of unconditional kindness to change people's lives.

How we walk with the broken speaks louder
than how we sit with the great.[v]

Bill Bennot
Author and Speaker

3

THE ANTIDOTE TO SHAME

At a critical moment in 2013, nine months after I had fallen and one month after I had repented, someone sent an anonymous gift to the chair of the trustees of my former ministry, *The Father's House Trust*. The letter included a cheque for about £1,000 to help me back on my feet again. Steve, my former chairman, told me that the man in question stated that he still believed in me, in spite of my fall. That comment, along with the generosity of the gift, was an act of great kindness.

And it was extremely timely.

In the weeks prior to this, I had sensed strongly that I needed to get myself to Bethel Church in Redding, California. The senior pastor there, Bill Johnson, was a good friend. He had come to St Andrew's Chorleywood a number of times when I had been the vicar there and described me as his first and best friend in the UK. Bill was and is a man I love and respect very dearly. He and his church felt like the right place, indeed a safe place, for me to get my life back together, so I was praying for the means to travel out to California and to receive some prayer.

Having lost everything, I was now completely broke, but when the money came in from the unknown donor, I was suddenly able to book airfares, a cheap hotel, and a place for the Leader's Advance Conference. In May 2013, I boarded a plane at Heathrow, arrived at San Francisco airport about twelve hours later, picked up my hired car, and drove the four hours up the freeway to Redding, where I fell exhausted into my hotel bed.

I was ready to move on from repentance to restoration.

True Friends

One of the things I will never forget about that week in May 2013 was the way in which Christian friends simply showed up and gave me the gift of their presence, despite the fact that it was well known that I had fallen.

Tim Eldridge was the first. Tim and his wife Sue are old friends. I had spoken at their conferences in Harrogate many times and had always enjoyed time with their family. Tim saw me on my first morning and asked me out for breakfast. He sat with me over Eggs Benedict, checking that I was okay, offering his unconditional love and support.

"Why don't you come and stay with Sue and me in Harrogate, when you're ready?" he said.

Tim's reassuring words, along with the excellent food, began to work on my troubled soul. I felt a measure of peace returning for the first time in many months. I sensed the possibility of a calm normality in my heart. Maybe it wasn't all over. Maybe I would get a second chance to live, laugh, and love again.

The following November I drove up from my mother's house in Wantage, where I was living at the time, to the beautiful northern town of Harrogate, just after the Christmas lights had started to throb with colour. The Christmas market, one of the finest in the UK, had been set up, and Tim, Sue, their dog Dibley and I walked through the busy pathways between the stalls, eating turkey and stuffing rolls and quaffing hot drinks. We talked and we laughed. During the rest of the weekend, we found our way into pubs and cafes and talked at length and in depth about my future. At no point did they want to dwell in judgment on my past history. They were only interested in my future destiny.

And in all the meals and the conversations, a tiny pinprick of light began to appear at the end of the very dark tunnel of my life.

It was called hope.

The Gift of Honour

Tim and Sue modelled something life-changing to me in those months, something counter-cultural and counter-intuitive, something heavenly, in fact.

It's called the gift of *honour*.

To honour someone is to value them not on the basis of their achievements or looks, but on the basis of their extraordinary value in the eyes of a loving, compassionate, kind and accepting Father.

Honour looks past the imperfections and flaws that mar our appearances, our reputations, and looks right into the soul, seeing the treasure hidden in the darkness, the thing of beauty and value that will outlive the ugliness and disgrace.

This requires an other-worldly way of looking at people.

It requires a divine paradigm shift.

Those who look at others through the lens of honour are truly the children of the Kingdom of heaven, because heaven is "a culture of honour".

When we look past a person's failure and penetrate beyond their shell of shame to the core of their personality, when we choose to stop judging what presents outwardly to our senses and move beyond that to the light within their soul, then we are closer to the Father's heart than we can possibly imagine.

When the prophet Samuel met the man that God had chosen to be king, the shepherd boy called David, he did what the Father always does. He looked beyond the young man's unpromising credentials and gazed instead upon the boy's soul. Why? Because the prophet knew that this is the Father's heart: to evaluate people not on the basis of outward appearances, but by looking into a person's heart.

That, in fact, is the essence of what it means to be a prophet. As the prophet Jeremiah declares, if we can see the precious in the worthless, then we become qualified to speak on behalf of the Lord (Jeremiah 17:15, NASB).

That is what Tim and Sue modelled. They offered me not only their time, which would have been a great gift in itself, but they offered me the gift of honour. They chose not to look on my past history, knowing that I was dealing with that in what would become a two-year course of intensive counselling. Instead, they kept their eyes on the Father's love for me as his precious, adopted son. They looked at my value in heaven's eyes and, in the process, became the Father's instruments of *kintsugi*.

The Way of Magnificence

Perhaps no story illustrates the *kintsugi* mindset more vividly or poignantly than the one involving Sen No Rikyū. One day, Sen No Rikyū was invited to the house of a Sakai tea man who had managed to acquire a particularly beautiful Chinese *chaire* – a jar for pouring thick tea. He wanted an opportunity to show it off. Who better to praise it than the most famous man associated with Japanese tea ceremonies in the sixteenth century, Sen No Rikyū?

The day came and the host duly used the jar to pour the tea for Sen No Rikyū and his other guests. However, Rikyū appeared not to notice it. The host waited and waited. Perhaps the man simply hadn't seen it. He made the jar more obvious. Still there were no words of praise for it from Rikyū.

After the tea ceremony, the host was beside himself with disappointment. Once his VIP guest had left, he was furious. In a fit of rage, he threw the perfect jar against an iron trivet. It shattered and the pieces fell to the ground.

The story goes that the remaining guests collected the fragments and later glued them back together using a special lacquer, *kintsugi* style. The repaired jar was brought back to the tearoom.

A short time later, Sen No Rikyū returned once again to the house as a guest. On entering the same room, his eyes were drawn to the repaired jar, its cracks filled with golden lacquer.

He smiled at the Sakai tea man who had been so desperate for him to praise the perfect jar a few weeks earlier.

"Now, the piece is magnificent!" Sen No Rikyū cried.

It's a great story, isn't it?

But it doesn't end there.

Many years later, another man bought the same restored jar for 1,000 golden pieces. Considering the repairs too crude, he took it to the most famous tea master of his day, Kobori Enshū, and asked him to make it more beautiful.

"You have missed the point," Enshū said. "The rough repairs are what made the piece so beautiful in the first place."

The man got the point and kept the jar as it was.

From then on, the restored tea jar was referred to as *o-meibutsu* – an object of fame – and it became part of the collections of many Japanese leaders and tea masters throughout the following generations.

Rikyū used this story to make a general point about restored vessels: "Tea jars that have been repaired with lacquer become even more fit for use."

Illusory Perfection

I think you'll agree, Sen No Rikyū presents a very radical, even subversive, way of looking at objects. He turned his gaze away from the jar with its illusion of perfection. His head was only turned once the jar had been broken and then restored. Only in its repaired form was the piece to be regarded as 'magnificent'.

How different this is from the Western Church today. Many churches have become conformed to the cult of celebrity. They build big, shiny congregations, led by people with extravagant haircuts and expensive suits. Everything is about appearance. The tea jar must be perfect, the pot flawless, the vase unblemished.

But this is so dangerous.

Trust me, I know.

This kind of Christianity merely reflects our worldly culture, it does not redeem it. Worse still, it sets people up for a fall. By idolising people, we build them so far up in our estimation and theirs that we all become consumers of appearance rather than devotees of reality.

This can have *catastrophic* consequences.

Many gifted men and women become Christian celebrities – a term that really should have been designated an oxymoron (a contradiction in terms) by now.

They are pushed higher and higher, and indeed push *themselves* higher and higher, until like Icarus, their waxen wings soar too close to the sun.

The fall is inevitable.

The celebrity, once flavour of the month, now crashes into the sea, making a bigger splash in failure than ever they did in so-called and apparent success.

And once they're down, how people love to gloat.

"They'll never minister again," people say. "It's over for them."

Rubber-Necking Religion

There's a particularly nasty habit to which most of us, if we are honest, are vulnerable. You know what I'm talking about. When we are on the motorway and the traffic slows almost to a halt. Neon signs on the hard shoulder alert us: "Accident Ahead", maybe adding further details, "Debris in the road". Our curiosity is piqued. What has happened?

When, sometimes after several hours, we draw alongside the scene of the accident, instead of passing by at a sensible speed and offering up a prayer for those involved, we slow right down and look at the mangled remains of what once were fine-looking cars. We search among the detritus for the injured, trying to assess the level of human injury, the extent of the misery amidst the trauma of the wreckage.

Then, as we pass by on the other side, many people start the inevitable process of judgment.

"They were driving too fast."

"I bet someone was looking at their mobile phone."

This is called rubber-necking.

The best do not engage in it.

They pray for the injured.

They say, "That could have been me."

The worst of us, the majority in fact, gawp and criticise.

This achieves nothing on the motorway, even less in the Church.

When preachers fall, the worst of us start rubber-necking the carnage of their lives. We stop what we are doing and Google their names, searching for more and more information. We may try and contact them personally, offering the pretence of compassion, while in reality hankering after details of the car wreck that is their lives. Journalists, both Christian and otherwise, are particularly prone to necking the rubber in this regard.

However, the best of those who follow Jesus are not like this.

The best say, "There but for the grace of God, go I" – something said to me after my own fall by two of my closest Christian friends. Both men, both with challenging marriages, both of whom had come closer than anyone will ever know to a car wreck like mine.

The best say, "I'm so sorry for my part in pedestalising you, Mark, and for helping to create a mythical version of who you really are." That was said to me by a Christian friend who used to invite me to speak at his conference every January, and by one of my publishers, with whom I had published over ten books.

The best seek for meaning in the mess by praying for healing and restoration for all concerned, for all caught up in the fall, including themselves.

The best are not deceived by the illusion of perfection, nor are they overawed by the aura of celebrity.

No, the best are *kintsugi* people.

They pray for the fallen person to be restored and for their family to be helped and healed.

The best cheer the fallen person on as they get back on their feet.

The British Way

I must be careful not to generalise, but this is not very British. We British don't tend to cheer the fallen when they rise. We tend to gloat when they're down.

After my fall, a dear friend of mine, an African American pastor, was speaking at a conference in the USA. One of the other speakers was an Englishman, someone who had invited me many times to speak at conferences in his church. When the two of them found out that I was a mutual friend, they began to talk about me.

"It's such a shame Mark is British," the Englishman remarked.

"Why so?"

"In the UK, we are very hard on the fallen. It's nearly impossible for them to ever be accepted again, even after they have gone through a process of repentance and restoration."

"That's so true," my African American friend said. "In the UK, you condemn people when they fall. Here in the States, we cheer them on when they rise again."

As it happens, I discovered for myself how true this is when in 2014 I was invited to the USA to lead a weekend workshop for Christian writers in Rhode Island. The event was hosted by a mainly African-American church where I had spoken many times. I'm giving a shout out here to New Dimension Apostolic Center!

I arrived at the venue at a time when the leadership team was going through a particularly difficult moment. The pastor, an old and dear friend called Theresa, invited me to the senior leadership team meeting to help them through the turmoil.

"Are you sure?" I asked. "It's one thing for me to lead a writer's workshop. It's quite another to offer counsel to your leaders. Do you think I'm ready?"

"Yes, I do!"

On entering the meeting, a huge bear of a man called Pastor Robert approached me with tears in his eyes.

"I only need to know one thing," he said before he held me.

"What's that?"

"Have you yielded to a restoration process?"

"Yes," I answered.

With that, he hugged me, then ushered me to sit at the head of the table.

Perhaps you can see what I mean when I say that the British have a special challenge when it comes to fallen people. The British delight in keeping people down. My American friends delight in helping people back to their feet, cheering when they do.

Are we among those who condemn those who fall, or are we among those who celebrate those who rise?

If you're among the latter, you're a *kintsugi* Christian.

And *kintsugi* is a Kingdom artform.

In the *kintsugi* mindset, true beauty is revealed in brokenness, not in the veneer of flawlessness.

In the Kingdom of God, true beauty arises when our Father, the divine Potter, takes hold of us in the honest and sometimes humiliating experience of our failure and then, far from hiding our scars, brings them into the light with the gold of his healing and redemption.

And that's worth cheering.

The Profumo Syndrome

In 2006, British politician John Profumo died. Profumo is infamous in British political history because he made one terrible mistake. It was a mistake that became headline news, one which led to him resigning from Harold Macmillan's government.

Married to the actress Valerie Hobson (star of one of my favourite British comedy films, *Kind Hearts and Coronets*), John Profumo was Secretary of State for War. In 1961, he had an affair over several months with a call girl named Christine Keeler, who was at the same time having a relationship with Yevgeny Ivanov, a Russian spy.

When the scandal came to light in 1963, Profumo lied to Parliament about it. He resigned from office on 5 June. I was 3 years old at the time. Growing up, I often heard his name mentioned, usually in hushed and embarrassed tones. His fall not only ruined his career, it also brought down the Conservative government. The following year, Harold Macmillan lost the general election.

Many of you will already know this part of the story. What you may not know is that for the rest of his days Profumo lived a quiet life, away from the public eye, bearing his disgrace with dignity, giving himself to forty years of charitable service to the poor in the East End of London. So great was his kindness to the down-trodden that Margaret Thatcher was to call him "one of our national heroes".

Why am I telling you this? Because this, to my mind, is another manifestation of the British way. When a person falls from grace in British life, it has traditionally been the case that they disappear to live a life of total invisibility, serving the poor as a penance for their sins. In no sense do I want to disparage working for the poor. Quite the opposite, in fact. All I'm pointing to is a kind of expectation embedded at one time within the British psyche. When a person with public influence is found guilty of a great failure, justice must be served, and justice means incarceration if the failure is criminal, and 'community service', as it were, if the failure is moral.

This traditional expectation is particularly strong in the Church, which is highly ironic when you consider that it is becoming less and less prevalent in wider society, where non-churchgoing people are generally much more compassionate. Even in 1963, a group of women in Profumo's constituency complained to those who had handled his resignation, saying, "He was popular here. We loved him. We'd have worked to get him back. What a d***d sanctimonious lot you are."

It seems that when it comes to restoration, society is sometimes more enlightened than the Church.

Indeed, one of many questions the Church needs to ask is this: does our thinking stem from the mind of Christ or from worldly notions of respectability, particularly those associated with elite boarding schools?

What if the culture of heaven is lightyears away from this?

What if a person can be truly forgiven and beautifully restored when they are genuinely remorseful?

What if they do not then need to live every day with a sense of shame, but with the knowledge that they are honoured?

What if we were to celebrate when the fallen get to their feet with the Father's help?

Derek Redmond – Again!

In my book, *The Father You've Been Waiting For*, I tell the story of British athlete Derek Redmond. I'm going to tell it again here, because it's profoundly relevant in a book for the fallen.

It was 1992 and Derek Redmond was running in his final Olympic Games. This was his last chance to fulfil his lifetime ambition to compete in a final at the world's greatest athletics event.

Kneeling at the starting blocks in the 400 metres semi-finals, Derek Redmond readied himself in front of the huge Barcelona crowd. The gun fired. He was off, heading down the track, building up speed.

Derek only needed to finish in the first four to qualify for the final. To many watching, it was a forgone conclusion.

Except that on the final lap something terrible happened.

Derek heard what he thought was a starter pistol going off, only it wasn't a pistol. It was his hamstring. It had snapped.

He pulled up and then fell.

The crowd uttered a collective gasp.

Everyone behind Derek now passed him, running round two bends, then down the final straight, crossing the line.

His dream was shattered.

Derek Redmond got to his feet.

He started hobbling.

Then hopping.

As he approached the final bend, a short, stocky man in a white T-shirt and a Nike cap clambered over the low wall separating the crowd from the competitors. The cap had a statement emblazoned on it: "JUST DO IT!"

The older man jogged onto the track, brushing security guards aside.

"I'm his father, Jim Redmond," he shouted.

The spectators in the stadium were now on their feet.

Jim Redmond put his arm around his son and began to walk him towards the finishing line, supporting him all the way, taking the pressure off his son's disabled leg.

As they crossed the line, it is said that the ovation they gave the father and his crippled son was louder than for any other winner in the entire course of that year's Olympics.

Afterwards, Jim was asked why he came to his son's aid.

"We started this thing together," he remarked, "so I thought we should finish it together too."

A few hours later, a Canadian competitor at the Games wrote this to Derek:

Long after the names of the medallists have faded from our minds, you will be remembered for having finished, for having tried so hard, for having a father to demonstrate the strength of his love for his son. I thank you, and I will always remember your race and I will always remember you – the purest, most courageous example of grit and determination I have seen.[vi]

What a story! And what a picture!

For those of you who are fallen, get up again! There is great courage in simply standing again. You may think you're a loser, but as soon as you get up from the track, you become a winner. Remember, the Greek word Nike means 'champion'. So quit thinking like a victim and start acting like a victor!

For those of you watching from the sidelines, don't criticise or condemn the fallen man or woman. Cheer them on as they get going again. Let the stadium of faith be a judgment-free zone. Let it be a place where those fractured by life and shamed by failure receive a resounding ovation when they rise up from the tracks, their veins filled with gold.

And for those of you called to help the fallen, be like Derek's dad. Be a walking, talking expression of the Father's love. Don't give those who have fallen a sermon; give them a shoulder. Help them to finish what they started.

And to all of us I say, JUST DO IT!

Early One Morning

The reason I believe *kintsugi* is a Kingdom art form is because this is precisely what I see in Jesus of Nazareth, who brought the Kingdom of heaven to earth 2,000 years ago. I see this very vividly in John 21, after Jesus has risen from the dead, when he returns to restore the fallen Peter.

There are so many things I could and will point out during the course of this book, but what I want to emphasise here is the way that Jesus does not give up on Peter. He does not treat Peter as a disposable commodity, someone to be replaced by, say John, the Beloved Disciple. No, he sees the precious in the worthless. He evaluates Peter on the basis of what's in his heart, not what's in his history. He honours Peter. He values Peter. He cherishes Peter.

How do we know? Here are the first words of John 21:

Afterward Jesus appeared again to his disciples, by the Sea of Galilee. It happened this way: Simon Peter, Thomas (also known as Didymus), Nathanael from Cana in Galilee, the sons of Zebedee, and two other disciples were together. "I'm going out to fish," Simon Peter told them, and they said, "We'll go with you." So they went out and got into the boat, but that night they caught nothing.

What's going on here? Peter has gone back to what he knows: his fishing business. He feels disqualified by failure, so he reverts to what is safe, familiar, and fulfilling. He invites six friends to go fishing with him. He does this because shame has a terrible tendency to make you want to isolate yourself, so human company is either avoided (the introvert reflex) or sought after (the extrovert reflex). For Peter, it is the latter, which is why he will not go out to sea alone.

Jesus seeks Peter out one morning, just as the sun rises. He is not here for the six friends. Although they are all of great worth to Jesus, they have not been guilty of a great moral fall, as Peter has.

Jesus makes an appearance for just one man. A fallen man.

That's how much he honours him.

The devil wants to convince Peter that it's all over and that he's on his own. His friendship with Jesus is ended.

Jesus, on the other hand, wants to tell Peter that this is just half-time. There are lessons to be learned, yes. But the second half is about to begin. All Peter needs to do is open his heart to the healing and cleansing process of restoration.

All Peter needs to do is admit that he's a broken pot and submit himself to *kintsugi*.

The Empathy Factor

Why is Jesus so moved to honour Peter in this way? There are probably many reasons but I'd like to highlight just one – empathy. Jesus doesn't empathise with Peter in his fall, because we know that Jesus was tempted as we are yet he never sinned (Hebrews 4:13). Jesus empathised with Peter because he knew what it was like as a leader to be targeted intentionally and specifically by a vicious enemy who wants to rob you, kill you, and destroy you.

Let's dwell on this for a moment.

I know from my own experience that those Christian leaders who make a stand for truth and justice never have a comfortable life. The more they confront various principalities and powers, the more the darkness is stirred up against them and against those whom they love. The darkness does not rage against the apathetic. The darkness rises up against the passionate. Those who, in Christ's name, seek to be truth-tellers in a hostile world.

Those who have the courage to speak out are nearly always assaulted in one particularly insidious way. The words they speak are the key here. The darkness swirls like a grim tornado around the heart of their message, seizes the words they have uttered, then sends demonic assignments that have one nefarious and destructive purpose: to undermine the message by bringing the messenger into disgrace.

This is precisely what happened to Simon Peter.

What was it he said?

His message, spoken to Jesus and the disciples in John 13:17, was this: "I will lay down my life for you."

Jesus replies, "Will you really lay down your life for me? Very truly I tell you, before the rooster crows, you will disown me three times!" (John 13:38).

How is Jesus so sure? The answer is given by Jesus himself in Luke 22:31-32, when he tells Peter that the enemy has a specific assignment to bring Peter down:

Peter, my dear friend, listen to what I'm about to tell you. Satan has demanded to come and sift you like wheat and test your faith. But I have prayed for you, Peter, that you would stay faithful to me no matter what comes. Remember this: after you have turned back to me and have been restored, make it your life mission to strengthen the faith of your brothers.

(PBT)

Peter's declaration was, "I will lay down my life for you, Jesus." The darkness heard this message, took hold of it, and swarmed around Peter when he and Jesus became separated in the courtyard of the high priest's house. When Peter was alone, the darkness undermined the message by assaulting the messenger. And as soon as Peter had failed to live up to his words, the cock crowed three times.

This is the reason why Jesus had such empathy for Peter. He knew first-hand how it felt to be targeted and undermined. He knew what it was like to be in the path of a demonic twister. He understood.

Jesus stood with his Father, and stood up for his Father's message, and for that reason, the enemy came hard after him, seeking to destroy the very heart of the message by destroying the very heart of the man.

He did exactly the same with Peter, and Jesus knew this.

This discernment was the source of his kindness towards Peter, the wellspring of his honour.

Peter fell, yes.

But he was also felled.

Never forget that.

It was Peter's choice to deny Jesus three times, yes. But he was also the victim of a vicious demonic assault. And while that can never be an *excuse* for Peter, it is a *reason*. It is a reason for his failure. And it is a reason for us to empathise with him.

It is a reason for us to be compassionate towards those who are felled for making a stand in their generation.

So then, be kind.
Be discerning.
Be like Jesus.

Honour and Subversion

When you show up with unconditional love and give the gift of your presence to someone who is fallen, you are performing the role of a *kintsugi* master in the Kingdom of heaven. You are, in short, being like Jesus to them, making them feel honoured in their shame and valued in their disgrace. You are saying, without using words, that they are not finished, not by a long way.

Look at John 21:4: "Early in the morning, Jesus stood on the shore."

What was he there for?

To spend time with just one man – Simon Peter.

What motivated him?

The value and honour he felt for Simon Peter, in spite of his fall.

What was his plan?

To cook some breakfast on the beach and to talk with Simon Peter in the context of a fireside meal.

What was his reward?

To see Simon Peter restored like a broken pot, by the kindness of heaven, which alone produces repentance.

Fresh Fire

I want to give a shout out to some other kind people at this point. I'm referring first of all to Adam and Rachel Graves and the fine people of FreshFire Church, Manchester.

After my fall, the first person in the UK to invite me to speak at their church – the first of a few, even to this day – was Adam Graves. Adam saw that I had begun a new business called *Kingdom Writing Solutions,* dedicated to helping good writers become great authors in the Kingdom of God. He invited me to come and lead a workshop for Christian writers in the Manchester area. I remember being really touched and humbled by this. Here was a man, and indeed a church, that was prepared to welcome me with open arms. Here was an opportunity for me, with faltering steps, to speak again. I was terribly nervous and wrestled with feelings of shame. But his kindness helped me to break through and speak again.

I shall always be grateful to Adam and Rachel. And to others too.

My old friend, Tony Collins, who had published so many of my books when he was working for *Lion Hudson and Monarch Publishers,* took me out to dinner twice during the first year after my fall. As did Malcolm Down, another old friend, another publisher of many of my books.

Both just showed up.

They were kind.

They were non-judgmental.

They sent love to me from their publishing teams.

They looked and sounded like Jesus.

And their kindness inspired me to want to get back on my feet again, with a repentant and restored heart.

To Adam and Rachel, to Tony, to Malcolm, I want to say a huge thank you. You played your part in my restoration in ways that you will never know until we all meet before our Father in heaven; the divine Potter, who specialises in repairing the countless broken cups and jars in his Kingdom on earth.

An Unexpected Call

When I was at my lowest, in the spring of 2013, a very kind woman called Alison Barr contacted me by email. She wanted to take me out to lunch in Oxford and talk to me about writing a book.

The email surprised and even shocked me. Alison was a senior commissioning editor for the largest Christian publishing house in the UK.

"Don't you know what I've done?" I asked, referring to my fall.

"Yes, but I still want to have lunch with you," she replied.

A week later, we met in a restaurant.

"Is there something you feel passionate about?" she asked. "Something that you've not yet written about? Something you'd like to publish with us?"

I couldn't believe what I was hearing. Not only was Alison giving me her time and buying me my lunch, she was also offering me a book deal. I had considered it unlikely that I would ever be in a position to write a Christian book again. The publisher thought otherwise.

I thought for a moment and then talked about a subject that I had started to explore and speak about before my fall, about the Cross and our adoption in Christ.

"Write a synopsis for me," she said. "I'll take it to the editorial team."

I went home utterly amazed, bewildered by the kindness and honour I had just been shown.

The next morning I wrote a pitch and within a week I had a book deal. The result? *My Father's Tears: The Cross and the Father's Love* (SPCK, 2015).

I am often asked which of my books is my favourite. The answer I always give is *My Father's Tears*. I wrote it in a time of immense pain, when I was living closer to the Cross than at any other time in my life. I wrote it when a Christian publisher told me that I was not disqualified as a writer, and that they wanted a book from me, having never published any of my books before. I wrote it because, in brief, someone showed me honour when I was feeling most ashamed.

And that honour contained within it a power more subversively transforming than any stern words of rebuke, or harsh words of condemnation.

The power of kindness.

For a broken pot like me, that meal was another *kintsugi* moment.

Cherith Adds

"When we honestly ask ourselves which person in our lives means the most to us, we often find that it is those who, instead of giving advice, solutions, or cures, have chosen rather to share our pain and touch our wounds with a warm and tender hand.

The friend who can be silent with us in a moment of despair or confusion, who can stay with us in an hour of grief and bereavement, who can tolerate not knowing, not curing, not healing and face with us the reality of our powerlessness, that is a friend who cares."[vii]

Henri Nouwen

When I think of those who stood by me, there are two people I can't overlook and who I have to mention.

I met Saul and Rachel through Mark; they were Mark's friends, and yet they supported and helped me when I was on my own. They owed me nothing, we had no history, but they were there for me every step of the way.

On the day Mark and I separated, Rachel and Saul were there. When I answered the door in tears, Rachel simply held me. She didn't say a word (which, for Rachel, is unusual to say the least!) They were there that day and they have been there ever since. They helped me move house twice, both times hiring a van and moving all my earthly possessions. Saul built and rebuilt Ikea furniture each time. They took me out for meals, we went to the cinema, and had wonderful chats in their house overlooking the sea.

Saul and Rachel made me laugh when I needed it most. They didn't use meaningless platitudes and empty words. They didn't try to come up with answers for questions I hadn't asked. I will never be able to pay these two back for all they have done for me. I have received so much healing just by being around them.

Sometimes, all broken people need is friends who show up and get stuff done. Just like Saul and Rachel did. In their own quiet and non-preachy way, they helped me along the road of restoration.

I always regard my creations as if they were my real children.[viii]

Genjuro the Potter
Ugetsu (classic Japanese film, 1953)

4

DON'T WASTE ANYTHING

In January 2013, I was at a critical moment in my life. I was out of work and languishing in a small flat, battling depression and fighting acute feelings of despair. I was in very real danger of losing any sense of purpose, any reason for getting up in the morning, and I was battling with my intense guilt and shame over what I had done four months before, on a Thursday afternoon in September. The weather outside was constantly drab, dull and grey; a mirror image of the state of my soul. Something needed to change, and quickly.

One night, a few weeks after New Year, I had a dream. This was something unusual for me; I never dreamed. Or, at least, I was never conscious of my dreams. But that night I had perhaps the most vivid dream of my life.

I was standing alone on a beach, looking out to sea. The ocean was calm and the skies were blue. All seemed well with the world. I felt as serene and peaceful as the sea.

Then, all of a sudden, the whole atmosphere changed.

The skies started to darken.

The wind picked up.

Thick, scudding clouds raced above me, heading inland, and with them, flocks of geese and other birds.

The sea started to head outwards, towards the ocean, as if sucked by a mighty and invisible force.

And then I saw it.

A mountainous wave, filling the horizon from left to right in the distance, as far as I could see.

A tsunami!

Except that it was unlike any wave I had ever seen, on TV documentaries, even in apocalyptic movies.

It was jet black.

Darker than the thickest darkness.

And right in the middle of the wave, extended in both directions, a word in huge, blood-red letters was somehow embossed on the water, heading towards me.

I N E R T I A

The font was striking too. It was jagged, like in movie or book titles for stories about serial killers.

It was utterly terrifying.

I looked to my right along the beach.

There was no one there.

Nothing.

I looked to the left.

Again, the place was deserted.

The only thing I saw was a small boat, more like a coracle, no more than six feet by six feet, with a waterproof skin that looked like it had been painted with tar, and a small mast in the very centre, around which was tied a burgundy, canvas sail.

At that moment, I knew I had a choice. I could either let the wave come on, break upon me, and destroy me, or I could grab hold of the craft and attempt something utterly foolhardy but at the same time supremely heroic.

In my dream, I seemed to possess a clarity that broke through the shock-induced numbness and fog of my daily waking life. I knew that to give into this inky wave, alluring as that thought appeared, would be suicide. My body would be found washed up on the beach and my story would end there. But what if I took responsibility in the moment? What if I behaved like a son, not an orphan, and made the brave choice, however reckless?

I ran to the coracle and pulled it towards what remained of the surf.

On and on I ran, dragging the flimsy craft behind me, until I reached some shallow water flowing out towards the incoming wave.

I climbed in and hoisted the sail as the boat was pulled towards the towering breaker, now cresting about one hundred feet above my head.

The boat started to ride up the base of the wave until I and the coracle were soaring up its front, through the great letters which dispersed as I touched them, up towards the top, the flimsy sail filled with a wind unnatural in its power and effect.

I was nearly at the top.

The noise was more deafening than a thousand waterfalls.

The sea fret was pouring off my face. The taste of it was on my lips.

Then, as quickly as I had reached the white fetlock of the wave, I was over the summit and heading down the other side, away from destruction, into a landscape of tranquillity – calm seas and breaching dolphins, blue skies and circling gulls.

It was over. I had made my choice in my dream. Now I needed to make it in my waking life.

Orphans and Sons

Even though I am a man of letters, I don't mind admitting that I had to look up the word 'inertia' the next morning. It wasn't one that I had ever used either in my writing or in conversation. A dictionary offered the following definition: "a tendency to do nothing or remain unchanged." That was a perfect summary of my life at the time. In terms of a job, I was doing nothing. In terms of my spiritual life, I was remaining unchanged. Something needed to budge. That something was me.

It didn't take me long to realise the implications. How often I had taught and written in the past about the difference between the mindset of the spiritual orphan, and the mindset of the son or daughter of God. Now it was time to apply my teaching in my own life.

Let me paint a picture of the person who has the heart attitude of an orphan.

The orphan has a spirit of entitlement. The orphan believes in passivity, not in taking active responsibility. The orphan believes that the world, God, society, owes them something. The orphan is lazy and greedy, hoarding things for themselves, not giving generously to others. Above all, the orphan is wasteful. Confronted by fracture and failure, the orphan does not seize the opportunity to learn from their mistakes and build a better, more healthy, selfless future. Instead, they allow themselves to be washed up on the beach, where they lie with the detritus from the ocean – human waste among all the other waste.

Now let me paint a picture of the son, the daughter, of the King of kings. I think you'll agree, it is far more empowering and far more enticing.

The son (and by son, I include daughters too, here) thinks and acts very differently. When tempted to embrace inertia, the son chooses to resist the pull towards paralysis. This is because in the heart of a son there is a spirit of entrustment, not entitlement. When a son experiences failure – as most sons do, if we want to be completely real – he does not give in to inactivity. He marches forward with whatever last vestige of heroism he can find within his wounded soul. The son knows that he has everything in trust from his heavenly Father. He knows that he is called to be a steward of this thing that we call life and he wants to waste nothing, not even the worst failure. So, the son gets up. He will not be ignorant of the lessons he could learn; the lessons he could give away with generosity to others. He will not allow his life to become wasted. He will not end up on the beach, covered in kelp. He will climb whatever mountain lies before him, knowing that, like Moses, he will find something glorious there.

This is the mindset of a daughter or a son. It is a mindset committed to spiritual growth and emotional health. It is the mindset that leads to *kintsugi*.

The *Mottainai* Cry

When Japanese ceramic artists first created the *kintsugi* method of restoring broken pots, it was something called *mottainai* that lay, in part, behind their thinking. *Mottainai* is a word that expresses regret over something that is wasted. It is what a mother will say to a child who is about to throw something away, something that could be recycled or put to another use. "*Mottainai!*" she cries. "Don't waste it!"

In the Japanese mindset, to waste something is to disrespect it. Japan is a land where, historically, resources have been scarce and where people have come to believe that everything has intrinsic value. That's the *mottainai* spirit, deriving from times when Japan was less affluent, now a vital part of Japan's psychology. It is this spirit that drives Japanese people to protect their natural environment. Indeed, *mottainai* has become something of a global rallying cry for those who are passionate about making green choices. For Wangari Maathai, an environmental activist, it is *mottainai* that lies behind his four R's:

1. REDUCE
2. REUSE
3. RECYCLE
4. RESPECT

While as Christians we may have questions about the spiritual roots of the *mottainai* philosophy – roots that are entangled with Shinto animism, and the view that objects have a spirit – there is no denying that this mindset is not only critical to saving our planet, it is also central to the practice of *kintsugi*.

When a favourite teacup or a priceless vase falls and is broken, the owner cries, either out loud or in their hearts, "*Mottainai!*" Nothing is to be wasted. The fractured pieces are gathered up and glued back together. The cracks are filled with urushi lacquer, coloured by gold dust. The result? A new teacup, a new vase, whose veins throb with the gold that was used to cure it.

And the good news is this: in the *kintsugi* mindset, the newly restored piece, with its fractures on display, is regarded as more beautiful and valuable than ever it was when it was flawless.

Toddler Spirituality

I have learned every failure is an opportunity to learn something revelatory that will help us grow up into people with a higher level of spiritual maturity and a deeper level of emotional health. I would go even further and say every failure carries within it the potential to learn truths about God, about ourselves and about life that we would rarely be able to access during times of ease and success. Sometimes the brightest light of revelation shines in the darkest moments of desolation. This is not a reason, nor an excuse, for pursuing failure, nor for falling morally, but it is one of the glorious things about the Father's love: we see and understand things in the 'far country' that we would be hard pressed to glimpse within the Father's house. Sometimes the pigpen yields up riches in the refuse.

Jesus knew this. This is why he showed up on the shores of the Sea of Galilee in John 21. He knew that there were lessons that Peter, and indeed the other disciples, needed to learn, that there was an enormous opportunity for growth in failure.

Where is the evidence for this? It is in a rather curious word that Jesus uses when he appears on the shore and calls out to the seven men in the boat. He doesn't use the word 'friends' as he calls for their attention. He uses the word *paedia* in Greek, which should be translated as 'little children'. *Pais* in Greek means 'child'. *Paedia* is the diminutive form of the word *pais* and should really be translated as 'infants'. Many of our English translations fail to capture this. They translate it 'friends', or 'children'. None, to my knowledge, dares to go the distance and render it 'little children' or 'infants'.

What a strange thing to shout to seven grown men! "Hey, you lot, you infants, you toddlers, it's me!" No wonder translators shy away from saying this, but they do so at great cost to what

Jesus is really trying to do here. In essence, he is trying to attract and incentivise his followers to grow up in their relationship with *Abba*, Father. He is trying to show them that failure is not the end of their development, the *terminus* of their walk with him, but rather the springboard for attaining greater maturity spiritually and deeper wholeness emotionally.

Infants No More

When I look back on my years growing up, they offer a useful picture of what I believe is going on here.

In 1960, my twin sister and I were *orphans*. We were left in an orphanage in London by a single parent mum who was unable to bring us up.

In 1961, we were adopted by Philip and Joy Stibbe and taken to their home in Berkshire. There we went from being *orphans* into being *infants*.

In the years that followed, Claire and I came to realise that we were the *children* of our adoptive parents. We already had that status, because of the legal adoption papers that were signed back in 1961, but we had to come to understand that even though we were born to another mother, Philip and Joy Stibbe were now our parents and we were their *children*.

This then led to us learning in time to acknowledge and revel in the joy of being a *son* and a *daughter* of these wonderful adoptive parents. This was not only our new identity, it was also our true inheritance. We were now *heirs*, not *orphans*.

A similar journey is undertaken by every person who repents of sin and chooses to put their trust in Jesus.

Keep in mind that the Bible says we are all the adopted children of God once we follow Jesus (Romans 8:15). Before this, we were spiritual orphans, separated by sin from the Father's love (John

14:18). When we came to Jesus, we turned from orphans to spiritual infants, drinking pure spiritual milk (1 Peter 2:2). Over time, we grew more and more into mature children of God, no longer drinking milk but eating solids (Hebrews 5:12). This then led to us living in the full freedom of sonship, revelling in our identity and inheritance (Galatians 4:4-6).

This is the life of every follower of Jesus. We go from being *orphans* to being *infants,* from being *infants* to being *children,* and from being *children* to being *sons and daughters* of God. Sons and daughters are those who have put all orphan traits behind them and who are now living like the one true Son of God by nature, Jesus.

All this takes time. And there are growing pains on the way.

Choosing to Grow Up

Perhaps you can see how extremely significant it is that Jesus, now raised from the dead, appears on the shore and shouts out "infants", or "little children", to Peter and his friends. They are behaving like orphans. They are running away from reality. They are living in denial. Peter, in particular, is seeking comfort in alternative affections: in his friends, his possessions, and his fishing business. This is always the way of the orphan, both the literal and the spiritual orphan. We end up worshipping the created rather than the Creator as a substitute for the one thing that will truly fill the void in our hearts: the Father's love. Driven by a desperate need to mask the pain of failure, we find people, objects and activities that we hope will make us numb to the agony within our souls.

It is this that Jesus comes to address in Peter, not in the harsh and judgmental tones of religious censure, but in the kind and compassionate tones of a perfect older Brother. Jesus appears on the shore not to condemn Peter, but to help him to grow to a new level of maturity and wholeness.

This, then, is the choice we all face after the fall. We can either hide away and live in denial, comforting ourselves with substitute affections. Or we can break out of this orphan mindset and grow up into healthy sons and daughters, ones who are more beautiful and valuable for having submitted their orphan hearts to the *kintsugi* restoration process of Jesus, who longs for us to leave our orphan ways behind, to develop beyond infancy and childhood into grown-up sons and daughters who bring pleasure to our Father.

Remember John 1:10-11, where John describes the purpose behind Jesus' journey from heaven to earth:

> He came to that which was his own, but his own did not receive him. Yet to all who did receive him, to those who believed in his name, he gave the right to become children of God.

Every fall is an opportunity to repent of our orphan ways and to grow up into wiser, healthier sons and daughters of God. And that is our choice, at every stage. We can choose whether to stay in sin or repent. We can choose whether to deal with our orphan traits or embrace restoration. The choice is always ours.

Butterfly's Wings

It is without doubt true that we have no choice when it comes to growing old, but we do have a choice when it comes to growing up. This holds in our spiritual lives too. We are going to grow older as Christians. The question is, are we going to grow up? Are we going to become healthier and holier? Are we going to become more mature? Are we going to grow into sons and daughters who look like Jesus?

After every fall, this is a choice, yes, but it is a choice made so much easier when the fallen man or woman is approached and assisted by people who exhibit the kindness of Jesus rather than the sternness of religion. The very worst thing you can do for a fallen person is come to them with condemnation for their past and despair for the future. For the most part, we already know we are sinners and we don't need that to be underlined. Furthermore, we already feel as if we are disqualified from having any future, so don't tell us that our only hope is a life of agonising penitence, devoid of the assurance of God's love. These things rarely, if ever, produce good fruit.

In other words, fear-based arguments are a very poor motivator for growth. They so often come from the mouths of people who wear masks, and they encourage mask-wearing in the person who is trying to embrace restoration. Fear does not motivate. Love motivates. Love is the only thing that will woo a fallen person out of their shame.

Here is what I have found from the stories of many other people. Make the fallen person feel worthy of love again and they will very likely change. Make them feel worthy of belonging again, and they will slowly break out of the chrysalis of sin and break free into the sunlight on butterfly's wings. This is the metamorphosis that we are all called to embrace. As Paul says in 2 Corinthians 3:18:

And we all, who with unveiled faces contemplate the Lord's glory, are being transformed into his image with ever-increasing glory, which comes from the Lord, who is the Spirit.

A Great Catch

Jesus is our role model here. When he comes to Peter in John 21, he comes to him with kindness. Kindness and *kintsugi* go hand in hand. Kindness is undeserved love, remember. Without the kindness of God, there is no repentance. And without the kindness of God, there is no restoration.

See how kind Jesus is to Peter in John 21. When Jesus shows up on the shore, he cries out "little children". Then he asks them if they've caught anything to eat that morning. The seven men on the boat, not realising that this is Jesus, reply "no". Jesus then tells them to throw their net from the right side of the boat. This is what John tells us happens next in John 21:6: "When they did, they were unable to haul the net in because of the large number of fish." Later, in Verse 11, we are told how many fish were in the net, and what kind: "It was full of large fish, 153, but even with so many the net was not torn."

This is something truly extraordinary! Jesus has given them a great gift – a huge number of large fish! Not one of these fish is lost. They caught 153 and they kept 153! Furthermore, the net is not broken, which is remarkable for such a catch. Jesus clearly believes in *mottainai*. He doesn't want anything wasted – fish or equipment.

And he clearly believes in abundance, in direct contrast to people with a religious spirit. He gives Peter the gift of an unprecedented catch, which is why I believe the number of fish is included here. There is no special symbolism in this number, as so many have tried to claim over the last two thousand years. It's a literal, not a figurative number. There really were 153 fish in one net, big fish too. And this was no fisherman's tale. There was no exaggeration. It happened. Fact!

But what's the point of all this? The point is that it is kind. Peter feels ashamed. He does not feel worthy of love or of belonging. But Jesus shows up and shows him extreme love in the form of abundant generosity. Rather than punishing him with poverty and threatening him with a hopeless future, he gives him a gift that says, "I still love you", and "You still belong!" For someone struggling with his orphan ways, Peter found this irresistible.

How different this is from the religious culture, which treats the fallen with sternness not kindness and advocates a life of scarcity rather than displaying heaven's generosity.

The Culture of Heaven

One of the reasons I am able to write this book is because wonderful people showed me shocking generosity after my fall. One man, a senior pastor, gave me a huge cheque to get me through a very tough time. A woman, a prophet, gave me a very generous cheque the same month. Another man bought a flat for me to rent by the healing breakers of the ocean, at a reduced, non-commercial rate. Over a year later, another couple bought my wife and I a cottage to stay in for as long as we needed it, again at a peppercorn rent. All these were acts of kindness and demonstrations of abundance. They facilitated our healing and they accelerated the process of growing up.

These acts of extreme kindness are the direct opposite of what we find in religion. These acts were motivated by Jesus, the King of kindness, the Master of *kintsugi*, and they were vital, critical moments in creating momentum in the restoration process. Without them, it would have taken me far longer than it did to come home into the Father's arms.

Religion is so different. Religion teaches the fallen that they must die a slow death, even after they have shed many tears of godly sorrow. Religion teaches the fallen that there is nothing but scarcity and poverty ahead, and these are the just rewards for our failures. The world of religion is accordingly the realm of the death camp. On its gates are emblazoned the words, "Abandon hope, all you who enter here".

Caution: Older Brothers!

When it comes to helping the fallen, we must accordingly guard our hearts from becoming like the older brother in Luke 15. He was outraged by the father's gifts of abundance to his younger brother: the robe, the ring and the new shoes. He was positively scandalised by the killing and cooking of the fatted calf.

I have learned from my fall that there are many like this, who have zero understanding that the Father's love is the diametrical opposite of what they believe and preach. The Father attracts our sinful hearts with kindness, honour and generosity, not with sternness, shame and misery.

Jesus is the exact representation of what the Father is truly like, and in John 21 he woos Peter out of his orphan state, not by the threat of scarcity and poverty but through the utterly undeserved gift of abundance.

And when it comes to the restoration of Peter, Jesus lights a fire and cooks some fish burgers, with sizzling and succulent meat from the fresh catch. In other words, he performs *kintsugi* during a feast, not a fast.

This is the Kingdom of God, the culture of heaven.

In this Kingdom, the heavy boulders on our backs become the stepping stones beneath our feet. They are mistakes, yes, but they are ones that we learn from in order to move on and grow up in our relationship with Jesus.

In this Kingdom, nothing is ever wasted, not even the greatest fall, the greatest failures. James Joyce said, "mistakes are the portals to discovery".

At least they can be, if only we overcome our inertia and take responsibility for own our mistakes, then learn from them.

To every person who is gazing with shock at the shattered pieces of their lives, Jesus cries from the seashore: "Little children, don't waste any of it!"

Cherith Adds

"God rewrote the text of my life when I opened the book
of my heart to his eyes."

Psalm 18:24 (The Message)

I came across this verse when I was studying English at university and I thought it was a beautiful translation and a lovely sentiment, but that's as far as it went. Today, this verse holds a world of meaning for me. I now edit manuscripts for a living and I am married to a man who writes books faster than I can proofread them!

I know that rewriting a text can take a long time; it is a precise and often arduous task. When people send their manuscripts through to us, they are sometimes apprehensive and nervous. Often, we are the first people to read their story and handing their 'baby' over to someone else can be a very vulnerable moment. However, a book will never reach its full potential unless it has been through this process and for that, it must be opened up to someone else's eyes.

This verse therefore requires us to act. God can bring beauty out of ugliness. He can turn our mistakes into miracles. But he won't do it without us opening up to him. This is the difference between a daughter who trusts her Father and an orphan who is afraid of what might happen if she allows herself to become vulnerable.

If someone trusts you enough to let you read their book, you count it as a privilege.

If someone opens their heart to you and allows you into their life, listen to them. Never underestimate the courage it takes for that person to allow you into their story.

Be kind, love them and allow God to do the rest.

Those who are willing to be vulnerable, move among the mysteries.[ix]

Theodore Roethke
Poet

5

PREPARING YOUR HEART

After my fall, I entered a period of shock for about six months. I walked around in a daze, bewildered by what I had done, even more bewildered by why I had done it. I survived for a while by shutting down my feelings, putting my entire emotional life in a self-induced coma. This numbing of the self was a survival mechanism I had learned from my boarding school days. The problem was that in shutting down my negative emotions, for a while I shut down all my emotions, including sorrow for my sins and a hunger for my Father's loving presence.

Eventually, something had to give. One Sunday morning, in February 2013, I was on my own sitting on a sofa. I had not read the Bible for a good while and prayer had been brief and intermittent. Something deep within my spirit was crying out for reconnection with my *Abba* Father, so I opened up a Bible reading app on my phone (*Bible in One Year*, by Nicky Gumbel) and read the Bible passages set for that day. As I did, the prayer in my heart was short but sincere. "Father, speak to me today, and whatever you say, I will obey." Then I started reading.

Within seconds, I was disturbed out of my emotional numbness. All three readings that day were on one theme: adultery. And all three were calls to repent – not harsh and condemnatory rebukes, but kind and understanding pleas.

That day, my emotions were reactivated and godly sorrow started to rise within me. And with that sorrow came another emotion – lovesickness. Lovesickness for the presence of God.

You could say I was travelling with King David, experiencing his heartfelt contrition over his sins in Psalm 51:

> Have mercy on me, O God,
>   according to your unfailing love;
> according to your great compassion
>   blot out my transgressions.
> Wash away all my iniquity
>   and cleanse me from my sin.
> For I know my transgressions,
>   and my sin is always before me.
> Against you, you only, have I sinned
>   and done what is evil in your sight;
> so you are right in your verdict
>   and justified when you judge.

In addition, I was crying out for my Father's presence, in the words of Psalm 63:1-3:

> You, God, are my God,
>   earnestly I seek you;
> I thirst for you,
>   my whole being longs for you,
> in a dry and parched land
>   where there is no water.
> I have seen you in the sanctuary
>   and beheld your power and your glory.

Because your love is better than life,
my lips will glorify you.

Ready for Restoration

In these months, I was being prepared for *kintsugi*. I was being made ready for a trip to the Potter's house, to receive the precious gift of restoration.

Everyone who goes through restoration goes through this process of preparation, and for everyone it is different. For some people, this takes a long time. For others, it is brief. For all of us, however, there is one thing that characterises every story, and that is desperation. All of us have to reach a point where we are desperate about something in the past (our sins), and desperate for something in the future (reunion with Jesus). The one is repentance, the other is restoration, and both are born from desperation in the soul.

To those who have fallen, I say this:

Give permission for your soul to feel desperate. When the Holy Spirit starts to stir your heart with sorrow, yield to that, even if it is only a hint. It is his divine wooing. It is his deep kindness. And when he starts to make your heart ache for the Father's arms, surrender to that too. It is the purest form of lovesickness that you will ever feel.

And to those who are genuinely called to befriend the fallen, I say this:

Do not force a fallen brother or sister into a place of sorrow and lovesickness. Let the Father do the wooing. Bow to his sovereign ways and his perfect timing. Any attempt to create such emotions in a fallen person's soul is religious manipulation and, at its worst, spiritual abuse. Just stand with the fallen. Be kind to them. Pray that they will grow into holy desperation when they are ready and the time is right. Don't force anything.

This is so important. Desperation is the soil in which restoration grows. But that desperation needs to be cultivated by our Father, who is the gardener (John 15:1). It needs to be prepared carefully, in the Father's good time.

Preparing for *Kintsugi*

Kintsugi masters know all about preparation. For a cup or jar to be repaired, everything has to be made ready; timing is everything.

First of all, there has to be a meticulous retrieval of every broken piece of the vessel. Nothing must be lost. Every shard is precious and must be reassembled.

There is a reason for this. *Kintsugi* tends to be practiced on tenmoku teacups. These are often very old, handed down from one generation to another. These tell a story. Their value to that household can never be measured in monetary terms. No wonder, then, so much care is taken in retrieving each broken piece.

Then, secondly, the lacquer must be made ready. This is the epoxy used to glue the fragments back together, so that the teacup can be restored and put on display, with a new story to tell.

The preparation of this adhesive substance is more of a ritual than a formula. The lacquer is made up of the raw sap from a local, deciduous tree, *toxicodendrum vernicifluum*. Also known as the Japanese Lacquer Tree, this has large fronds and grows to over 20 metres. The Japanese have known about the qualities of this sap for over 5,000 years. They have also known that this grey-yellow sap can only be removed through making an incision in the bark of a tree that is at least 10 years old. These incisions from the trunk must be made at the right time too, between the months of June and November.

Once this sap is extracted, it is subjected to a filtering process so that all the impurities are removed. It is heat-treated before gold dust (sometimes silver dust) is applied to add colour to the glossy sap. This highly durable and top-quality epoxy is known as *urushi*. It is what gives the restored teacup its golden or silver joins.

You Cannot Hurry

What a vivid parable of the preparation that must go into *human* restoration too.

Once again, we can marvel at Jesus, the Wonderful Counsellor and Prince of Peace, as he sets about the work of restoring Peter in John 21.

There is something we need to note about the sacred preparation of Peter in this story, and that is Jesus' patience. Jesus waits until Peter is ready. He does not rush the process or force the issue. There is no religious control here. No, Jesus leaves Peter for several weeks after the first appearance to his disciples in the upper room in John 20. He waits until Peter's heart is filled with desperation over his brokenness, and desperation for his healing.

What was Peter doing between the time of Jesus' first appearance to all his disciples in John 20, and the appearance he makes to Peter (primarily) and his six friends in John

21 on the shores of Galilee? I can tell you based on my own experience. Peter was wrestling with shame.

As I have written in many of my books, shame is different from guilt. Guilt is what you feel about something you've done. Shame is what you feel about who you are. Guilt is accordingly a doing word. Shame is a word associated with being, with my view of who and what I am.

There is no doubt that Peter felt guilty about what he had done. He was in anguish over his denials of Jesus. But more than that, he was ashamed of who he was. He saw himself as defective and disqualified, as fallen and a failure.

This kind of shame is toxic because it leads to isolation. It creates in us the feeling that we are no longer worthy of being loved, accepted and valuable to the cause we once embraced. Instead, we feel as if we no longer have the right to belong to those we had served. This causes us to hide from God, from others, even from ourselves.

For restoration to take place, the fallen person must be prepared to come out of hiding. They must become desperate – desperate to be forgiven for what they've done (the guilt issue), desperate to be accepted and loved again for who they are (the shame issue).

Those who are fallen need to wait for this moment when the pieces of their lives have been gathered up in the hands of the divine Potter, when the sap of holy healing has been made ready by the divine Gardener. That requires patience.

Those who are befriending the fallen need to be patient too. Their role is to keep being kind, and to keep praying that the Father will bring the fallen person out of hiding. This means warfare prayer and requires fervent intercession because the enemy of our souls is the father of lies, peddling the deception that we must forever hide. We all need to remember that the devil isolates, but Jesus integrates. In warfare prayer, we must call the fallen person out of the darkness and into the light, but only when that person is ready, when that person is truly sorrowful. Their desperation is the foundation for their restoration.

Hungry in the Desert

There is a transcendent beauty about the Father's love. It remains faithful to us, even when we are unfaithful. It remains committed, even when we wander. It remains tenacious, even when we let go of its dazzling affection. This love never surrenders, never gives up, never fails. This love just keeps on loving, even when the embers of our love are no longer glowing. This love keeps on wooing, even when we are not responding in the way that we should.

This is the love that burned in the heart of Jesus as he came, early one morning, to the shores of Galilee. This is the love that burned in his heart as he stood from afar watching Peter, just as he had done in the weeks prior to this moment, although Peter had never once seen him. This is the love that kept appealing to Peter's troubled heart, even while Peter was in hiding, even while Peter was trying to mask the pain in his soul by going out fishing with his mates. This love was vaster than the sea before which Jesus was standing. Here is love indeed, vast and deep as the ocean.

When Peter was in hiding in the desert of his shame, this love never gave up on him, never let go of him, never left him for a minute. Oh yes, Peter had sinned, and God hates to look upon sin. He is holy, blindingly holy, and we must never forget that. But he is also compassionate and his mercy, as the Bible says, triumphs over his judgment. His kindness supersedes his sternness. His love conquers all.

So, in the desert of his shame, Peter is not abandoned by the divine love. He is wooed by it. His place of isolation becomes his place of preparation. As Jesus, the Bridegroom, says of his Bride in Hosea 2:14-15:

> Therefore I am now going to allure her;
> I will lead her into the wilderness
>   and speak tenderly to her.
> There I will give her back her vineyards
>   and will make the Valley of Achor a door of hope.
> There she will respond as in the days of
>   her youth,
> As in the day she came up out of Egypt.

In the natural realm, deserts are where we become hungry. In the spiritual realm, things are no different. In the one, we ache for food. In the other, we ache for the Love of all loves, just as Peter did, just as every fallen person will, when they say yes to *kintsugi*.

Jumping at the Chance

There comes a moment in every person's life when preparation meets opportunity. For Peter, that happened early one morning when Jesus came to the seashore and called out to him and his friends. At first, Peter does not recognise who is speaking. But then Jesus tells them where to put their nets and they catch a large haul of big fish.

It is at this point that the Beloved Disciple, traditionally identified as the Apostle John, recognises who is calling to them. "It is the Lord!" he cries. Simon Peter's reaction is both fascinating and revealing in Verse 7: 'As soon as Simon Peter heard him say, "It is the Lord," he wrapped his outer garment around him (for he had taken it off) and jumped into the water.'

There are so many things I could say about this response by Peter. Let's just focus on two details.

First of all, please notice that Peter 'wrapped his outer garment around him'. What is Peter doing here? Some argue that Peter is wearing an undergarment, as was common for fishermen in those days. Hearing that it is Jesus calling, Peter puts on his outer garment before meeting him.

Others argue that Peter is wearing his clothes but they are loose to give greater room for his arms as he works among the nets. In their perspective, Peter *ties up* his garments.

I prefer the first picture, painted in the NIV translation. Peter puts on his clothes in order to meet Jesus.

That's an odd thing to do before jumping into the sea. Why does he do that? At least one explanation must be because, like Adam and Eve, Simon Peter felt naked and ashamed in the presence of Jesus.

Secondly, notice Peter's enthusiasm. We know that he is prone to being passionate. On the first Easter morning, described at the beginning of John 20, Peter races to Jesus' tomb. He runs hard and fast, but the Beloved Disciple outruns him and gets there first.

Peter will not allow this to happen again!

This time Peter dives into the sea before the Beloved Disciple even thinks of competing. And Peter gets to Jesus first, dripping with seawater and sweat, his heart racing at the exertions and, most of all, at the thought of seeing Jesus again.

This, I submit, is a beautiful picture of desperation. Over the weeks, Peter's heart has been made ready. He has become more and more eager to see Jesus. His heart is full of longing, aching for reconnection, docile to the Spirit, desperate for love.

Divine Editing

The same thing happened to me in the spring of 2013. Having repented, I was now living alone in a small room. All I owned in the world was in the back of an old, rusty estate car which I had borrowed from a friend.

It was in these months that I felt called to start a new business, helping Christian writers to publish their books. I called it 'The Script Doctor' (now 'BookLab') and pretty soon, God was calling people to send me their manuscripts to assess and edit. In fact, it was during these months that I went back to my first passion in life – writing. I went back to basics. Stripped of all the trappings of a successful Christian ministry, I slowly rediscovered who I truly am and what gives me the greatest purpose. Somehow, in all the ministry at churches and conferences, I had lost sight of my true identity and my real destiny. I had lost my love of books and needed to find that again. Editing manuscripts, dealing with mistakes and creating a more coherent text, became my joy. It also became a metaphor for my life.

As my hunger grew, I reconnected with my good friend Paul Manwaring, a Brit on the senior leadership team at Bethel Church in Redding, California. I shared with him my desire to return to Bethel for a visit and asked if he would help me. In one of our email correspondences, he shared a passage of Scripture:

God made my life complete
    when I placed all the pieces before him.
When I got my act together,
    he gave me a fresh start.

Now I'm alert to God's ways;
   I don't take God for granted.
Every day I review the ways he works;
   I try not to miss a trick.
I feel put back together,
   and I'm watching my step.
God rewrote the text of my life
   when I opened the book of my heart to his eyes.

Psalm 18:20-24, The Message

I don't think it's possible for me to describe my reaction when I read this unfamiliar version of a very familiar Psalm. I was astounded. Here was what I was longing for. My Father, the greatest author of all, was going to rewrite the text of my life as I opened the book of my heart to him. He was going to make my life complete and give me a fresh start so that I would feel put back together.

All I had to do was be desperate enough to place all the pieces before him.

Then, like a *kintsugi* master (if you'll forgive me mixing my metaphors), he would repair and restore my soul, and I would be alert to his marvellous ways.

That's what I was desperate for and, like Peter, I was ready to jump at every opportunity.

Cherith Adds

When Mark was reading those words about adultery in February 2013, he was experiencing the conviction of God. It felt so different from the judgement of others that he couldn't do anything other than listen. God's words to him were so full of love and grace. They ushered him to repent.

But I was far from ready to repent. Honestly, I was angry. When well-meaning Christians told me 'in love' to do what was right, I began to isolate myself. The problem was that in hiding from others, I also hid from God. A lot of people (including my church) had distanced themselves as far from me as they possibly could. Why would God be any different?

For a few months, I couldn't bring myself to read the Bible and I couldn't bear to listen to any worship music.

Through my choices and because of my sin, I had lost friends and, deep down, I was terrified of losing my heavenly Father too.

I didn't want to hear what He had to say to me.

Then, one weekend, I reached breaking point.

I needed God. I missed him.

In the past, God had often spoken to me through worship songs and hymns. I thought that would be a good place to start, so I fired up my laptop and started to listen. I was desperate to feel something; I was no longer comfortable being numb. But I felt nothing. Somehow I had moved beyond them and their words could no longer affect me. Maybe God was really done with me.

As my desperation grew, I heard the words of a song by *Tenth Avenue North* for the first time. The song, entitled 'Worn', speaks of making mistakes, but knowing that there is hope in the mess of a broken life. In the darkness of my struggle, this song, raw and real, provided a tiny flicker of light and I began to make my way home.

The song was like a modern-day Psalm. It held nothing back and as I listened to the words, neither did I.

I sobbed.

The defences I had built to protect my heart came crashing down and as they fell, God was there.

I cried because I was sorry and I cried because I was astounded that he was still there for me.

In my brokenness, God assured me that I was not beyond repair.

There is a crack in everything. That's how the
light gets in.[x]

Leonard Cohen
Poet and Singer

6

A FIRE BY THE SEA

In May 2013, I was given the opportunity to travel out to Bethel Church in Redding, California – what the Celtic saints would have called "a thin place". A thin place is one where the membrane between heaven and earth is so permeable that it almost doesn't exist at all. It is a place where angels walk among us. It is a place where healing comes, and quickly. It is a place where sinners are forgiven and the fallen are restored. Bethel is a quite wonderful church, rooted in the Scriptures, focused on Jesus, and filled with the Father's love.

When I arrived, I was exhausted physically, drained emotionally, and empty spiritually. In the months before my visit, I had undergone an intensive period of what I can only describe as *kenosis. Kenosis* means 'emptying', specifically 'self-emptying'. That is exactly what I had experienced. I was no longer concerned about my reputation, my status, my image. All that had gone. In fact, when religious people tried to condemn and criticise me, it had no effect. I used to say, "there's no point shooting a dead man. Don't waste your bullets. My desire for approval and my longing to measure up to your expectations are all gone. I'm a dead man walking!"

I arrived at Bethel at the start of one of their most important annual conferences – the Leadership Advance. The senior pastor, Bill Johnson, was exceptionally busy but he offered me an afternoon of his time. I went to his office and he asked me what I needed in terms of prayer ministry.

"You can have anything," he said. "I'll give you my best people."

I was overwhelmed by Bill's kindness. I felt then, as I have felt often since, that I was in the presence of Jesus.

"I'd like a *Sozo* session," I said.

Bethel Church run an inner healing and deliverance ministry called *Sozo* and I had heard from people I trusted and respected that it had helped them greatly during critical times in their lives.

"I'll arrange for you to see Dawna De Silva," Bill said. "She heads up *Sozo* Ministries here."

The next day I found my way to Dawna's office. After introducing myself and giving a very brief summary of my story, she looked at me and said, "We'll not do a step-by-step *Sozo* session, if it's all right with you, Mark. I think I'd rather invite the Holy Spirit to do whatever he wants."

I nodded.

She walked towards where I was sitting. "Is it okay if I put my hand on your shoulder?" she asked.

I nodded again. Then she prayed. As she welcomed the presence of the Holy Spirit, something began to happen. I felt this warm sensation starting at the top of my head, going down through my body, to the soles of my feet. I was bathed and cleansed in holy fire, through and through. It was a true *kintsugi* moment.

Feeling the Heat

When it comes to the process of repairing broken teacups, *kintsugi* artists know how important it is to involve heat in the process. In the last chapter, I mentioned how the preparation of the *urushi* lacquer – the glue that cements the broken pieces back together – involves heat. The raw sap needs to be heat treated before it can be applied.

The same is true, not just for the preparation of the lacquer, but the repair of the teacup itself. This process, in which the pieces become fixed together by the lacquer over time, also involves heat. The teacup, or the tea jar, needs to be given time before it can be put on display or used again. Timing is crucial, and so is temperature.

The drying process is crucial in *kintsugi*. Having prepared the gold-coloured lacquer, and having glued all the fragments together, the object needs to be placed in a heated environment. This is because *kintsugi* masters understand that the lacquer does not go through a normal drying process. It needs to be exposed to a heat source, one varying from 10 to 20 degrees centigrade, and kept at a relative humidity of 70 to 90 per cent.

Exposed to heat and water, the glue undergoes a chemical process in which it begins to harden and become water resistant. Often, the teacup or tea jar is placed in a special *muro* or box, with a small plate of water inside and a heat source nearby. The object must be kept warm and it must be kept close to water.

Burning Coals

As I write this, I find myself once again in awe of Jesus, the restorer of my soul. What does he do when he exposes Peter – that broken vessel – to the Kingdom process of *kintsugi* in John 21?

First of all, he addresses Peter's failures and fractures near water, specifically by the sea. This context is reinforced in the first half of the story:

Verse 1: "Afterward Jesus appeared again to his disciples, by the Sea of Galilee."

Verse 4: "Early in the morning, Jesus stood on the shore."

Verse 7: "As soon as Simon Peter heard him say, 'It is the Lord,' he wrapped his outer garment around him (for he had taken it off) and jumped into the water."

There's no mistaking the importance of the sea here. The sea for Peter was his safe place. It was the environment he had known as a child.

Once again, I marvel at the ways of God. I too was brought up by the sea, in North Norfolk. When it came to my own two-year process of restoration, much of that took place as I was living on my own in a rented flat overlooking the ocean. The sea was my safe place. The poet E.E. Cummings knew this too. He once said, "For whatever we lose (like a you or a me), it's always ourselves we find in the sea."

Jesus restored Peter by the sea.

But he also restored Peter by a fire.

The detail of the fire is critical in Jesus' masterful use of Kingdom *kintsugi* in John 21. Look at what John, who (as the Beloved Disciple) witnessed this entire restoration scene, reports in Verse 9: "When they landed, they saw a fire of burning coals there with fish on it, and some bread."

A fire of burning coals!

Why does Jesus light a fire, and specifically one, as John so precisely notes, of 'burning coals'?

The answer is stunning. The word that John uses for 'a fire of burning coals' is the Greek word *anthrakia*. The NIV translators rightly emphasise that this word refers to a charcoal fire, not any old fire. Why is John so specific?

In John 18, we see Peter denying that he knew Jesus three

times when he is questioned by a maidservant. Where is Peter standing when he makes these denials? By a fire. And not any old fire. This is a charcoal fire. The word is *anthrakia*, the same word that is used in John 21. *Anthrakia*, as I pointed out in my commentary on John, is only used twice in the entire New Testament: John 18 and John 21.

Clearly John has seen something very powerful about the context that Jesus chooses for Peter's restoration.

Jesus not only chooses a safe place (by the sea).

He lights a fire.

In doing this, Jesus establishes the perfect conditions for Peter's restoration.

This is sheer genius.

Jesus is truly heaven's *kintsugi* master, and John 21 is heaven's blueprint for restoring the fallen.

Jogging our Memories

By now, it should be clear why Jesus lights a charcoal fire. Yes, there is a practical reason: he wants to cook the fish. But there is a psychological reason too. Jesus wants the smell of the cinders, the sound of the fire, the heat of the flames, the sight of the coals, and the taste of the smoke to awaken Peter's memory of his failure. He wants to use the fire to stimulate Peter's senses in such a way that he will remember and not deny his denials.

This is awe-inspiring, at least to my mind, because it's only been in the last two centuries that we have come to understand the way in which an appeal to our five senses – touch, taste, smell, sight and hearing – can have such a profound effect on our memory. The writer Marcel Proust wrote about this in his famous and ground-breaking novel *In Search of Lost Time*, begun in 1909. At the beginning of the story the narrator, Marcel, dips a madeleine (a small cake) into a cup of tea. Straight away, the sensation transports him back in time to a moment when his Aunt had given him a similar biscuit, also dipped in tea:

> "No sooner had the warm liquid mixed with the crumbs touched my palate than a shudder ran through me and I stopped, intent upon the extraordinary thing that was happening to me. An exquisite pleasure had invaded my senses, something isolated, detached, with no suggestion of its origin … And suddenly the memory revealed itself. The taste was that of the little piece of madeleine which on Sunday mornings … when I went to say good morning to her in her bedroom, my aunt Léonie used to give me, dipping it first in her own cup of tea or tisane. The sight of the little madeleine had recalled nothing to my mind before I tasted it. And all from my cup of tea."[xi]

How appropriate, in a book about the restoration of broken teacups, that Proust should be talking about a cup of tea! What Proust is talking about here is IAMs, Involuntary Autobiographical Memories. These are aspects of an automatic memory process known as 'ecphory' (from the Greek verb, *ekphorein*, meaning 'to reveal'), in which cues in our surroundings align with events stored in our brains to evoke a particular memory, without the conscious effort of the one remembering it.

All this makes sense to me. The most terrifying day of my life was my eighth birthday. That was the day I started ten years at boarding school. I felt terribly abandoned and afraid. The teacher looking after me, as I waved to my departing parents, was a towering and untrustworthy man – presenting as one thing when my parents were present, quite another once they were gone. Later that evening, he stormed into my dormitory with a cane and thrashed my bare backside in front of all the other new boys, all for dropping a bag of marbles.

Today, if I visit a stately home, I have to be careful. The hall and stairs of my prep school were made of heavy oak and covered in a particular polish. If I smell that polish again, I am right back to my eighth birthday, standing in the vestibule of the country house, scared and alone.

Proust was right, suppressed memories can be triggered by aromas, but he was wrong in saying that it is only these sorts of cues that result in the awakening of dormant or suppressed memories. Objects can act as triggers too, and so can words, as we will see in Chapter 8, when Jesus asks Peter three times whether he loves him.

How brilliant Jesus is! He lights a charcoal fire in order to awaken shameful memories that need healing in Peter's soul. He does something that will only truly be understood 1,800 years later!

Jesus is truly ahead of his time, but then he is before time and beyond time.

What else should we expect from the great divine Potter and heaven's *kintsugi* Master?

Holy, Healing Fire

But we shouldn't stop there. The burning fire is not just a stimulus for evoking an involuntary autobiographical memory. It is also symbolic of something more, something transcendent, something utterly mysterious. It is a literal representation of a heavenly reality: the fire of divine love.

In the Bible, fire is a symbol of the manifest presence of God. Now I know what some of you are going to say: "God is omnipresent. His presence is everywhere. So what's with all this talk of his 'manifest' presence? How can he be more present than he already is?"

Ask Moses, would be my answer. Ask David. Ask Jesus. Ask John. Ask all of the Apostles. And specifically, ask Peter. They knew that God was present everywhere, that there was nowhere they could go from his presence. But they also experienced moments when that invisible presence was made visible, when the intangible was made manifest.

Moses certainly knew this. He saw a burning bush in the desert. The bush was on fire, but not consumed (Exodus 3). As Moses approached, God urged him to take off his shoes. In the Middle East, when you are invited to someone's home, your hosts tell you to remove your shoes. This is code for "make yourself at home with us". When God said "take off your shoes" to Moses, he was revealing divine love. He was saying, in effect, "Make yourself at home in my presence, Moses."

When Jesus lit a fire, there was more going on than just a barbeque. This moment was to be for Peter an encounter with the divine love – an *experience* of the healing, liberating flames of that heavenly love that will not let us go, that love that never gives up on us, the Love of all loves.

Incendium Amori

We all have our favourite writers. One of mine is the English mystic Richard Rolle (1305-1349). During his life as a hermit in Yorkshire, he wrote a very famous book called *The Fire of*

Love (*Incendium Amori*, in Latin). It was not a book for the learned. Rolle was not a trained theologian or an ordained priest. He was writing for ordinary people:

> "I offer ... this book for the attention, not of the philosophers and sages of this world, not of great theologians bogged down in their interminable questionings, but of the simple and unlearned, who are seeking rather to love God than to amass knowledge."[xii]

One of the reasons I love Rolle is because he clearly experienced what he called the fire of God's love. His knowledge of God was therefore not purely intellectual and conceptual; it was experiential and affective. Rolle experienced a kind of 'warmth' (*calor* in Latin) in his heart. He would have empathised with John Wesley, who 400 years later was to say, "my heart was strangely warmed."

For Rolle, Christianity was a spirituality of the heart, not just a religion of the mind. Look at what he says here:

> I cannot tell you how surprised I was the first time I felt my heart begin to warm. It was real warmth, too, not imaginary, and it felt as if it were actually on fire. I was astonished at the way the heat surged up, and how this new sensation brought great and unexpected comfort. I had to keep feeling my breast to make sure there was no physical reason for it! But once I realized that it came entirely from within ... I was absolutely delighted, and wanted my love to be even greater.[xiii]

What a description that is! Do you feel your heart yearning for this fire as you read it? Do you ache for an encounter with the fire of the Father's love?

Peter was to experience tongues of fire on the Day of Pentecost, just a few weeks later. For now, as the flames licked and crackled on the sand nearby, the warmth of the fire fused with the warmth of the love of God, creating a moment of encounter which would leave the fisherman repaired and restored, like a broken pot in the hands of the greatest of all *kintsugi* artists.

Back to Bethel

When I was being prayed for by Dawna De Silva in her office, I was desperate. I was like Peter. I jumped at the opportunity and crossed the sea to meet Jesus. In Dawna's office, Jesus lit a fire. Not a literal fire. That would have been catastrophic! No, this was the fire of love – a fire in which God brought hidden memories to light for healing, a fire in which he gave me total deliverance from chains that had bound me since the day I was abandoned as an orphan in 1960. A miraculous fire!

One day, I may write a full description of what happened in that encounter with the manifest presence of God. But for now, I will mention just one thing.

When I was a child, I used to suffer from a rather nasty condition. My ears would quite often become blocked by a build-up of wax. This was not only acutely painful, it also reduced my ability to hear what people were saying. Much to the irritation of my dear mother, who would often cajole me verbally to help with the washing up, or some other domestic chore, only to find that her commands fell on deaf ears.

So, off to the doctor we would go. And it was the same process every time. The doctor would fill a large syringe with hot water, then place it in my ear. The nurse would position a metal bedpan underneath my earlobe, and then it was all systems go. In went the hot water, I would wince with pain, then the relief would come at last as all the offending gunk would pour into the pan. My reaction was always the same. I would look down at the disgusting blobs in the water and think, *Has that stuff really been in my head all this time?*

The answer was yes. But it was out now, and I could hear again!

When Dawna was praying for me, this was precisely how I felt. It was as if the pressure and heat of the Father's love was simply too much for all the shadows in my soul, and they all came flooding out. And as I looked down afterwards, I thought to myself, *Has that stuff really been in my head all this time?*

Same answer – yes. And the same result too. I could hear again. I could feel the Father's presence and I could hear the Father's voice.

Jesus had lit a fire for me too.

I had smelt the memories that needed forgiveness and healing.

I had felt the heat of the divine love, and experienced a great release, a mighty deliverance.

Maybe it's time you asked Jesus to light a fire on the shores of your heart. As Richard Rolle knew, there is nothing quite like the fire of God's love!

Cherith Adds

I love how Jesus approaches Peter. There are some things that really move me about this passage. Jesus is careful and thoughtful in creating an atmosphere where Peter feels safe and familiar. Jesus is a safe person in Peter's life.

Mark's experience was tailored to his needs and experiences. He was in a place where he knew he was safe and he knew he could trust his friend. This created an environment in which he could receive healing. What would have happened if circumstances were different? Where do you go if the church rejects you?

That, to some degree, is part of my story. I have found that churches who accept broken people are everywhere, but churches who accept broken, fallen *Christians* are much harder to find.

As Christians, we make mistakes, we sin, and we are broken.

Too often when Christians fall, there is an attitude that says, "Well, they had their chance and they've blown it."

When Mark and I left, my church expressed a desire to distance themselves from me and my story. This left me in a predicament: on the one hand, I believed in church and I loved the community it provided, but on the other, I felt I wouldn't be welcome in church again.

I'd had my chance. Right?

My story of restoration began outside the Church. I had some *kintsugi* moments on my own in my little apartment near the sea, listening to music, talking and praying with friends on the phone and reading my Bible. I visited quite a few churches. Each time I had the same routine – I arrived late and left early, terrified that if anyone talked to me, they would realise I wasn't worthy to be there.

In the end, I gave up. Some of these churches may have been wonderful places of healing for broken people, but my fear born out of my previous experience got in the way.

Some years later, when Mark and I were married, we joined *Presence Church* in Harrogate, run by our friends Tim and Sue Eldridge. It became our safe place. This was the first time I had been part of a church that truly felt like family.

The wonderful people in *Presence* knew my story and accepted me anyway. This was so important. It is in the presence of God we are healed and restored and *Presence Church* lived up to its name. I felt welcome and free to be myself.

This did not mean what I had done in my past was deemed unimportant or somehow acceptable. 'Everyone welcome' is not the same as 'anything goes' and even in my darkest moments I did not expect – or even want – this kind of attitude.

I believe that healing and restoration is as much for those who walk with God as it is for those who don't know Him.

I believe that we need to be better at admitting that when we believe in God it doesn't make us perfect or sinless.

Our churches should be workshops where the golden lacquer of *kintsugi* art is used most freely, and the place where 'broken pots' feel most loved.

If we can share our story with someone who responds with empathy and understanding, shame can't survive.[xiv]

Brené Brown
Author and Speaker

7

THE MAGNIFICENT SEVEN

As I navigated the choppy and sometimes turbulent waters after my fall, I was so grateful not to be alone on the journey. Even while I was living in solitude for long stretches, I was never abandoned. I had the support of my own family – my brother and twin sister stand out – and the support of loving, Christian friends. These friends in particular were crucial to my restoration. I want to mention two of these.

I had known Hugh and Ginny Cryer before my fall, having spoken several times at conferences in Winchester, where they had been the senior pastors of a Vineyard church. Later, they started a new ministry called Culture Changers. At that time, I was helping an author who knew them well. He showed me Ginny Cryer's excellent book, *Culture Changers*.

One chapter in and I was hooked. This was everything I had ever wanted Church culture to look like. It was rooted and grounded in the Father's love, centred on Jesus, and devoted to the Holy Spirit – 'the empowering presence of God', to use my late friend Gordon Fee's term. More than that, Ginny argued that the Church now needed to live as a family of adopted sons and daughters of a perfect Dad. They were truly singing my song.

A little while later, I met Hugh and Ginny in their house. As we sat and drank coffee, Ginny asked if I sensed the powerful presence of God amongst us. I smiled and said yes. We then waited on the Lord, realising that His presence was the affirmation they had needed for His approval of our friendship.

Within weeks, I was having dinner with some of their friends in Culture Changers. Within months, I was part of the Culture Changers' team.

One thing that struck me was the way in which both Hugh and Ginny understood how God sometimes accelerates grace, especially when it comes to restoration. Over the next two years they watched over Cherith and me as the Lord restored us, they observed our genuine repentance and growing spiritual hunger. All this then led them, with complete integrity, to ask if they could prepare us for marriage.

Hugh and Ginny not only acted as witnesses at our legal ceremony at a registry office, but later in 2015 led the prayers for us at a joyful celebration and blessing of our marriage at a beautiful country house chapel in West Sussex. In the latter, Hugh walked Cherith down the aisle, standing in for her dad, who was unable to travel from Northern Ireland due to a serious foot injury.

Today, Hugh and Ginny are a spiritual Dad and Mum to Cherith and me. They have walked with us through the tough as well as the good times.

They are, in a word, *family*.

A Family Affair

My point here is this: when it comes to restoration, the fallen man or woman must never be left to go it alone. They need people around them who are committed to supporting them, to cheering them on as they get off the floor, brush off the dust, and learn to stand again in the presence of the Lord and his people. Restoration doesn't happen to a person in religious, solitary confinement. It happens in a loving, Christian community.

Let's look ("at last", some might say) at the use of word 'restore' in the New Testament. The Greek verb is *katartizo*. You can find it thirteen times in the New Testament and often in two ways. The first, I call 'occupational'. In this first sense, 'restore' is used in the context of fishing and refers to the mending of broken nets. Here's Matthew 4:21-22:

> Going on from there, he [Jesus] saw two other brothers, James son of Zebedee and his brother John. They were in a boat with their father Zebedee, *preparing* their nets. Jesus called them, and immediately they left the boat and their father and followed him.

The word italicised should really be translated 'mending' or 'fixing'. After every fishing trip, fishermen would check their nets to see if there were any breakages. If they found any, they would restore the nets in preparation for the next fishing expedition, hence the NIV's preference for the translation 'preparing'. 'Mending', I think, would be more accurate, which is what you find in the KJV.

The second context for 'restore' is *ethical*. Here it refers to mending people rather than mending nets, specifically, helping those who have fallen into sin to get up again. Here's Galatians 6:1:

> "Brothers and sisters, if someone is caught in a sin, you who live by the Spirit should *restore* that person gently."

In this passage, the italicised word refers to a compassionate mending of the fallen person's soul. That this restoration is meant to be undertaken by kind and humble people is reinforced even more clearly in The Message version: "If someone falls into sin, forgivingly restore him, saving your critical comments for yourself. You might be needing forgiveness before the day's out." That is a very sobering translation!

Clearly, New Testament Christians prioritised the task of restoring their brothers and sisters. They did not leave the fallen behind. They were not like soldiers who simply ditch their wounded, leaving them in the mud by the side of the road as they go marching on. No, they gathered around the fallen person, as fishermen gathering around broken nets. They sought to offer loving support, guiding their broken brother or sister into wholeness and holiness, helping them to be refined by their mistakes, not defined by them.

In this endeavour, the role of the community was, and is, supremely important. When we see the nets being restored in Matthew 4, the process is undertaken by members of the same biological family: Zebedee (dad), John (son), and James (son). When we see people being restored in Galatians 6, Paul addresses 'brothers and sisters', highlighting the fact that restoration is the task of a spiritual family – the Church!

Restoration is never achieved when the fallen person is isolated. That is abandonment. No, it is achieved in a context of genuine, family love.

And only when the Church begins to function as a family will it become a safe place for the fallen.

Into the Tearoom

It is here, once again, we can learn so much from the Japanese art of *kintsugi*. When vessels such as teacups are broken, the shattered pieces are not left on the floor, nor are they swept quickly into a bin. They are gathered up, every piece, even the tiniest. They are looked after carefully. They are then prepared for a process of restoration by a *kintsugi* master, or a group of *kintsugi* masters, who devote considerable time and energy to the undertaking, sometimes spending over a month restoring one object so they can return it to the owner, who will honour the repaired cup as if it was a brand new work of art.

All of this traditionally took place in a tearoom. Keep in mind that the tearoom and the tea ceremony are important parts of traditional Japanese culture. Since the fractured teacup or tea jar was a priceless expression of this tradition, the tearoom was the perfect place for its restoration.

The Church, once again, has a lot to learn from this. When our brothers and sisters fail and fall, they need a safe place and they need safe people for their restoration. There is no safer place than a home where that fallen person feels totally accepted, even if their loved ones disapprove of what they have done. This safe place can be the home of someone in our biological family. It can be the home of someone in our spiritual family – someone like Hugh and Ginny Cryer!

And don't forget the importance of tea! If you don't like tea, substitute something else. I am talking about family meals, cups of coffee, beach barbeques, anything that conveys the message that a person is loved, that a person belongs. That is essential if the healing is to begin.

That is why I am so grateful to Hugh and Ginny, as Cherith is. We have had so many healing moments at their kitchen table. We have shared so much food and drunk so much coffee together.

There is a lesson here.

Bring the broken teacup into the tearoom.

Let the *kintsugi* begin!

A Meal with a Message

Jesus knew all this. When it came to the restoration of Peter, he established a safe place. He lit a fire on the seashore and cooked some of the fish that Peter and his friends had just caught. He then invited them all to sit and eat with him, not just Peter. Here is what John says in Verses 13-14: "Jesus came, took the bread and gave it to them, and did the same with the fish."

It is so important to notice how many people took part in Peter's restoration. There was, of course, Jesus. In addition, there were the six friends that Peter had invited to go fishing with him at the start of the story. In Verse 2, the full complement of fishermen is mentioned: "Simon Peter, Thomas (also known as Didymus), Nathanael from Cana in Galilee, the sons of Zebedee, and two other disciples were together." In total, there were seven men on the boat: Peter and six of his friends, all of whom were fellow disciples of Jesus.

This is revealing. When it comes to Peter's restoration, the whole process is witnessed by Jesus and by six of Peter's friends.

This makes *seven* witnesses.

Seven is the number symbolising perfection in Jewish thought. Seven is the perfect number of witnesses to a fallen person's restoration, just so long as those seven people are part of the Jesus family, as it were.

In Jesus' eyes, restoration must occur in a safe place, such as a meal. It also needs to be attended by safe people – people like

Thomas, for example, who in the previous chapter (John 20) had himself undergone a process of healing during a personal encounter with the risen Jesus.

Safe people are kind people, and kind people are empathetic people.

They have their own scars.

They understand.

The Role of Witnesses

In Chapter 4, I wrote about how following Jesus involves spiritual growth. We go from being spiritual orphans to being spiritual infants, from being spiritual infants to being spiritual children, and from being spiritual children to being the spiritual sons and daughters of the living God.

In this process, *adoption* is absolutely critical. I have written extensively about our spiritual adoption in Christ for over twenty years. Books of mine like *Orphans to Heirs* introduced many Christians to this theme for the first time. Since then, other writers have followed my lead and written about it too.

It was the Apostle Paul who taught that when we come to Jesus, we are adopted into a spiritual family in which God is our *Abba*, our Daddy, and Jesus is our perfect older Brother. As a Roman citizen, Paul had seen childless Roman parents adopt children. Most often, the child in question was a slave, and the process involved a ceremony performed in front of a Roman magistrate in which the child was bought three times by the adopting father. Paul saw this and thought, *What a picture of our salvation! We have been bought out of slavery, not by gold or silver, but by the precious blood of Jesus. We have a new adoptive Papa too! And we are now no longer slaves but sons, with a new father, a new freedom, a new family, a new future, and indeed a new fortune – the incomparable riches of amazing grace!*

The best known passage of Paul's on adoption is Romans 8:15: "The Spirit you received does not make you slaves, so that you live in fear again; rather, the Spirit you received brought about your adoption to sonship. And by him we cry '*Abba*, Father.'" This was one of John Wesley's favourite passages and he preached on it frequently during the eighteenth century revival in Great Britain. But note the verse afterwards: "The Spirit himself testifies with our spirit that we are God's children." Here Paul talks about the Spirit of God as the one who witnesses our adoption.

William Barclay, in his commentary on this passage, makes this observation:

> The adoption ceremony was carried out in the presence of seven witnesses. Now, suppose the adopting father died and there was some dispute about the right of the adopted son to inherit, one or more of the seven witnesses stepped forward and swore that the adoption was genuine. Thus the right of the adopted person was guaranteed and he entered into his inheritance. So, Paul is saying, it is the Holy Spirit himself who is the witness to our adoption into the family of God.[xv]

How many witnesses were there?

In the Roman rite of adoption, there were seven.

How many people witnessed what was going on when Peter was restored?

Seven!

A magnificent seven!

Every fallen person needs to commit themselves to spiritual maturity by getting up after their failure and resolving to grow up into a son or a daughter who is more whole and more holy than before.

Every fallen person needs safe people who can act as witnesses of their restoration, especially if their restoration is questioned. They need enough witnesses in case it is questioned years after the event.

Every fallen person needs to be set free from their orphan chains, understanding that adoption is not just a one-off event in their past, but a process that lasts the whole of their lives.

As I have often said, "The Christian life is one long journey of inner healing, punctuated by moments of deliverance." In this long journey, we need witnesses to the integrity of our decisions. We need our own version of the magnificent seven! We need family – true family.

The Importance of Writing

We should never forget that one of the seven witnesses of Peter's restoration was the Beloved Disciple. Throughout the last 2,000 years, many commentators and Bible interpreters have identified this man as John the Apostle. John was a fisherman by trade and had been called by Jesus, along with his brother James, and indeed Simon Peter, to follow him after the miraculous catch of fish described in Luke 5. This had taken place about three years before, right at the start of Jesus' ministry.

Once John was sold out for Jesus, he changed over time from being a fisherman to being a writer. In all likelihood, he probably wrote not only the Gospel of John, but also the three letters attributed to John, and the Book of Revelation –

a series of visions that he was given while he was in chains on a remote and rocky island called Patmos, imprisoned there by the Romans. Even there, he exercised his writing gift. The chains couldn't hold him down. Jesus had said to him, "Write what you see in a book" (Revelation 1:11). No power in hell or on earth was going to stop him.

Why am I emphasising this point? It's because one of the witnesses of Peter's restoration took the trouble to exercise his writing gift and record the way in which Jesus so kindly and so insightfully helped Simon Peter back onto his feet. His record has stood the test of time. It is part of the world's bestselling book (the Bible) and the Church's most-loved Gospel. For all ages, John has recorded what he witnessed: the beautiful work of heaven's *kintsugi* master, Jesus Christ, as he spent time with a fallen man and not only put him back together again, but put him back on his feet.

There are two ways in which I have applied this in my own life.

Firstly, I have taken the trouble to tell the story of my fall and restoration. A record has been made of the way in which Jesus took the broken pieces of my life and brought me to a place of wholeness. This book is a tribute to the extraordinary way in which my Father creates integration out of disintegration, and turns our mistakes into miracles. There was much to celebrate in this, and I simply had to write it down so that others – either the fallen, or those who help the fallen – could be encouraged.

Secondly, I quickly saw that I needed to include faithful witnesses who saw what Cherith and I went through as we travelled the arduous journey from fall to recovery. They are mentioned in this book, and their commendations were the only ones I wanted when it came time to publish. These friends are my equivalent of 'the magnificent seven' in John 21.

So then, don't ignore the role that writing can play. John wrote a record of Peter's restoration. I have written the record of my own restoration, and Cherith has added her reflections about her journey too. And most importantly of all, we have the words of those who have shown us such extreme kindness, such Christ-like love, and who have collaborated with Jesus in taking the fragments of our lives and restoring us to a beautiful new usefulness with the gold of God's love.

Let there be a witness to what you have experienced and learned. Let there be a record of God's goodness. As God says in Habakkuk 2:2: "Write down the revelation and make it plain on tablets so that a herald may run with it."

Cherith Adds

"The friend in my adversity I shall always cherish most. I can better trust those who helped to relieve the gloom of my dark hours than those who are so ready to enjoy with me the sunshine of my prosperity."[xvi]

Ulysses S. Grant

I have some wonderful friends who stood by me when it cost them dearly to do so. They each served a different purpose in my healing journey and I'm just sorry I'm not able to mention them all here. I'm going to pick out two of those friends and tell you a little about them. I pray it challenges all of us to see the beauty in those who sometimes do ugly things.

Rachel

Rachel and I have been friends since high school. We went to university together and, apart from Mark, she is probably the person who knows me best. In one of my early chats with Rachel after my fall, she said something which has never left me: "Cherith, I'm so sorry you felt like you couldn't tell me what was going on."

I found it hard to process this statement. I should have been apologising to her. I realised that I could have talked to Rachel but I made an incorrect assumption about her reaction.

I've thought a lot about this over the years and I've come to the following conclusions:

1. We need to be better at letting our nearest and dearest know that they really can talk to us about anything. This

alone could save lives.

2. As broken, messed up people, we need to try to be a little braver and talk about the mess with those people who truly care for us.

3. Everyone needs a friend like Rachel!

One of the most important things Rachel did for me was remain unchanged. She treats me the same way now as she did when we first met – no judgement. Throughout my restoration, this sense of normality was so important. Having said that, our friendship is deeper and so much more precious the other side of my fall.

I will forever be grateful for her unwavering loyalty.

Juliette

After Mark and I had parted in 2013, during the many months I was living alone, I had weekly phone calls with Juliette. Juliette is a Christian counsellor and she gave me one of the greatest gifts I have ever received – she listened without judging.

I poured my heart out, I cried, I told her everything. As we chatted, I often found myself being more real with her than I had been before, even with myself. Sometimes we would pray together and as we did, I felt my face turning slowly back towards my heavenly Father. Juliette's role in my restoration was key; although she never said these words explicitly, every chat we had whispered, "You are loved. It's going to be okay."

Those chats were my church for months and I'll never stop being thankful for Juliette, who took time out of her busy week to talk to a 'broken pot'.

And what did you want?
To call myself beloved, to feel myself
beloved on this earth.[xvii]

Raymond Carver
Short Story Writer

8

A GRIEF OBSERVED

On 4 March 2013, Cherith and I knelt and prayed. We knew we had sinned before God and wounded those whom we loved. With tears pouring down our faces, we repented of our fall and laid our relationship down. With godly sorrow, we surrendered everything to the Father and then went our separate ways, Cherith to move to a flat on her own, me to a tiny room in a kind stranger's home. As far as we knew, that was it. All we could pray was, "Your will be done."

I don't think I have ever shed as many tears as I did that day. We both knew we were doing the right thing, but that didn't make it any easier. On that March morning, as I drove away from our flat in Ashford, all I knew was this: Cherith and I had been confronted by a tough question. "Do you love each other more than you love me?" Neither of us could answer yes. We both knew, in the deepest recesses of our souls, that we had always prized one thing above all else – the Father's love. In both the good times in the Father's house, and in the bleak times in the 'far country', we had treasured one thing more than anything – the knowledge that we were, and are, infinitely loved by the best Dad in the universe. We had felt ourselves beloved on the earth by a good, good Father in heaven, and nothing could take his place.

So, I drove away, my face red with tears. For one who had suppressed his emotions for over four decades, it was as if someone had flipped a switch and I simply couldn't stop crying. Even the bright Kent sunshine – so often a source of elation – could not comfort me. My sorrow over what I had done was overwhelming.

Later that evening, the two men who were overseeing my repentance at the time (one involved in my former ministry, the other a local pastor), posted online a public notice expressing Cherith's and my contrition over what we had done, and the hurt we had caused, using words that I had written and they had agreed.

That was the day I died.

Broken Teacups and Lost Coins

At this point, I want to say something again about *kintsugi*, that I'm conscious that the analogy fails. Why? Because broken teacups don't shed tears.

There is a view linked with *kintsugi* that inanimate objects have spirits, but this is not supported by the Bible. As with all analogies, then, we must be respectful. While there are so many similarities, we must be careful not to obliterate the differences. When teacups fall to the floor and break, they do not feel the pain of their fall, nor do they weep over the sorrow the damage has caused to others. Teacups don't have souls. They don't have tear ducts. They don't have emotions.

Jesus understood this. He knew that only human beings are capable of feeling grief over their sins. This is one of the main reasons why Jesus tells three stories, not one, when in Luke 15 he wants to explore the limitless vistas of his Father's amazing love for the lost.

In the first story, he tells of a lost sheep. When the sheep is found, the shepherd rejoices, and calls all his friends and neighbours to rejoice. The Father rejoices too in heaven. Emotions are on display everywhere, except, of course, in the sheep, who feels no sorrow over wandering off and getting lost, who sheds no tears of repentance over its reckless actions.

In the second story, the lost object is even more impoverished in its emotional register. Now Jesus talks about a lost coin. When the owner eventually finds it, after sweeping and searching her entire house, she rejoices, and her neighbours rejoice. Again, the Father rejoices in heaven. The coin, meanwhile, has been singularly unaffected by the entire experience. It did not weep when it was lost and it did not leap for joy when it was found.

And Jesus knew this!

Which is why he tells a third story, completing the divine trilogy.

This time it's a boy who is lost.

This time it's not just his dad who feels so deeply and strongly about the eventual heart-warming reunion. The boy does too. He is bereft in the 'far country'. Back home, in the father's house, he is literally speechless with joy, bedazzled by his father's love. He wanders around the party being held in honour of his return, bemused by the astonishing forgiveness he has been shown. He gathers the festive, honoured robe around his shoulders. He holds his signet ring up to his friends, its metal glinting in the sunlight. And he shuffles around the barbeque in his new leather shoes, yet another gift from his father.

Teacups do not shed tears of repentance.

Nor do sheep.

Nor do coins.

But boys and girls do. Men and women do, when they come home to the scandalous generosity and outrageous kindness of the world's greatest Dad, because we know, in our brokenness, just how astounding it is to be accepted by the Love of all loves. As theologian Paul Tillich once said:

> Grace strikes us when we are in great pain and restlessness. It strikes us when we walk through the dark valley of a meaningless and empty life. It strikes us when our disgust for our own being, our indifference, our weakness, our hostility, and our lack of direction and composure have become intolerable to us. It strikes us when, year after year, the longed-for perfection of life does not appear, when the old compulsions reign within us as they have for decades, when despair destroys all joy and courage. Sometimes at that moment a wave of light breaks into our darkness, and it is as though a voice were saying: 'You are accepted.'[xviii]

I simply don't know any better definition of grace than that. In our tears, we feel beloved on earth by our Father in heaven.

And that is amazing grace.

Simon Peter's Grief

Peter encountered this grace when he met Jesus by the Sea of Galilee in John 21. As Jesus spoke to him, he began to shed tears as he owned what he had done.

The scene is described with beautiful simplicity and remarkable restraint by John in verses 15-17. After Jesus has fed the fishermen, he turns to Peter and addresses him alone. As you read the scene, keep in mind what I wrote earlier about the way in which we remember our past not only through triggers like smells and sounds, but also through words.

> When they had finished eating, Jesus said to Simon Peter, "Simon son of John, do you love me more than these?"
> "Yes, Lord," he said, "you know that I love you."
> Jesus said, "Feed my lambs."
> Again Jesus said, "Simon son of John, do you love me?"
> He answered, "Yes, Lord, you know that I love you."
> Jesus said, "Take care of my sheep."
> The third time he said to him, "Simon son of John, do you love me?"
> Peter was hurt because Jesus asked him the third time, "Do you love me?" He said, "Lord, you know all things; you know that I love you."

There has been so much said and written about this passage over the years, particularly about the different words Jesus uses for love. He not only uses *agapein*, which means to love someone self-sacrificially, but *philein*, which means to love someone affectionately, like a friend. I personally believe that people make too much of these differences. I believe there is something else to consider here, the way in which Jesus addresses Peter *three times* with the question, "Do you love me?"

This, as many people have pointed out, is clearly intentional. Jesus wants Peter to stop suppressing his grief over the denials. He wants to call him out of his denial of the denials, if you will. To do this, he uses various cues that are carefully designed to evoke the memory of his failure. The first is the smell of the charcoal fire, which takes Peter back to the courtyard where he denied Jesus. The second is a verbal cue. It is the fact that Jesus asks Peter three times, a clear echo of the three times that Peter had denied that he was a disciple.

What is Jesus doing here?

He is helping Peter to reconnect with his emotions.

Jesus wants to know if Peter still loves him more than anything or anyone else. More than he loves his friends. More than he loves his job as a fisherman. More than he loves his possessions – his boat and his nets.

He wants Peter to reveal his heart.

He wants to hear from Peter's own lips that there is no love in his life that eclipses his love for Jesus.

And he wants to see Peter's grief over what he has done.

And Peter is sorrowful.

As John records, Peter was hurt. Why? Because Jesus asked a third time, and that reminded him of his three denials.

With that, Peter confronts what he has done and the grief over his fall begins to surface.

Blameless, not Just Holy

For some Christians, particularly those who have a suspicion of emotions and a deep-seated fear of inner healing, all this talk of "getting in touch with your feelings" will be quickly dismissed. For them, restoration is simply a matter of repenting at the Cross and being obedient to God's Word.

It is that, but it is far more than that too. As long as we tell fallen people that all they need to do is increase their commitment to spiritual disciplines like prayer, they will always be vulnerable to falling again. This is because we have hearts as well as spirits, and a purely 'spiritual' solution will not suffice when we have wounds that lie deep and dormant in our hearts, ready to erupt like a volcano. Emotional healing is needed too, and for that we will very likely need counselling. Through counselling, we get past 'what we did' to 'why we did it'. When we address the why, and let the Healer do his work in that deeper, more visceral part of the soul, then we stand a chance of rising up as healthy and mature sons and daughters, ready to serve again.

When the Apostle Paul talked so passionately about our adoption in Christ, he made it clear that we were predestined to become the sons and daughters of God for one great reason – to be holy and blameless in the Father's eyes (Ephesians 1:4-5). Please notice that Paul uses two words here: 'holy' and 'blameless'. What is the difference between these two adjectives?

The first word, 'holy', means morally pure. It means living an alternative lifestyle – the lifestyle of the Kingdom of heaven, as opposed to one conformed to this world. For that to happen, we need repentance in the root sense of the word. In Greek, repentance is *metanoia* which means a U-turn in the way we think about things. For adopted sons and daughters of God, this means embracing a new mindset – the mindset of Jesus. Once we have the mind of Christ on all matters of personal and public morality, we think differently and then we act differently. This is because what we believe radically affects how we behave.

The second word, 'blameless', means something different. It is the word that was originally used for the lambs slaughtered at Passover. They were to be perfect in this one sense – that none of their bones were to be broken. What is the implication of this? If 'holy' means morally pure, 'blameless' means emotionally whole, no longer fragmented, no longer fractured. The adopted sons and daughters of God need to be both morally holy and emotionally whole. If restoration is to be effective, we need a holistic perspective.

And this is what we see in Jesus' restoration of Peter in John 21. He is not only interested in Peter becoming more holy. He is also interested in Peter becoming more whole. Like a *kintsugi* master, everything needs to be gathered up. All the fragments must be reintegrated in the Father's love, because in his Kingdom, everything gets repaired and restored – our spiritual, moral, physical, emotional, and relational lives. As the Welsh poet and priest R.S. Thomas wrote, in his beautiful sonnet about the Kingdom of God:

> It's a long way off but inside it
> There are quite different things going on:
> Festivals at which the poor man
> Is king and the consumptive is
> Healed; mirrors in which the blind look
> At themselves and love looks at them
> Back; and industry is for mending
> The bent bones and the minds fractured
> By life. It's a long way off, but to get
> There takes no time and admission
> Is free, if you purge yourself
> Of desire, and present yourself with
> Your need only and the simple offering
> Of your faith, green as a leaf.[xix]

When Memories Awaken

The truth is, we have a choice. When bad things happen to us, or when we do bad things to others, we can either bury the memory or we can deal with the suffering we have received or inflicted. The problem is, it is human nature to want to avoid and to anaesthetise our pain, whether that is the pain done to us by others, or the pain we have received from others. Our natural reflex is escape and avoidance. So we suppress our memories of the wound, with all the shame that attends it.

In November 2016, Channel 4 newsreader Cathy Newman asked to see me. She mentioned that it was about someone called John Smyth, who was an evangelical barrister in the late 1970s and early 1980s. She said that it would be off the record, if I wanted, but that she was working on a story about his abuses of boys and young men who had attended a Christian summer camp run by the Iwerne Trust (now renamed Titus Trust) between 1978-1982.

When her email arrived, it threw me into turmoil. I had not talked about this man for many years. Her words awakened the traumatic memories – memories not only of being groomed and abused by John Smyth, but memories of the damage he had done to my closest friends at school and university. Principal among these was my dear friend Andy Morse, who tried to commit suicide in February 1982 in order to avoid being abused in a horrifically savage way.

All these things I had suppressed for 35 years.

When they came out in the public domain, first on Channel 4 and then on BBC1, the memories began to resurface from the ocean depths. One by one, they emerged as I reconnected with Andy and others, and as I shared my story with trusted people.

Now, having brought all these memories to Jesus, I no longer feel shame. I have dealt with the pain. I have confronted the full effects of John Smyth's influence on my life, especially the catastrophic consequences on my relationship with my first wife and my children, to whom I have apologised. Above all, I have forgiven my abuser. He no longer holds me captive in my bitterness. I am free!

The Power of our Tears

When we connect with the pain of what we have done, or what has been done to us, it hurts – as Peter discovered. It does bring tears to our eyes. But when these tears begin to stream down our faces, they hold immense power. Every tear is accompanied by a sigh, and these sighs are the wordless prayers of the adopted sons and daughters of God – prayers that ascend to the courts of heaven, filling golden bowls around the Father's throne. When our Father sees these tears and hears these sighs, he cannot help himself. His heart bursts with pleasure at our intercession and with pity at our desolation. What ascends from earth as a sigh is returned from heaven as lightning.

When Cherith and I went to the European Leader's Advance in Harrogate in the summer of 2016, we heard one of our heroes speaking. We both love Heidi Baker because she is not only a modern-day Christian mystic, she also has the most amazing heart for orphans and for the poor generally. Her ministry in Africa is characterised by mercy and miracles. We wanted to hear Heidi and we were not disappointed.

At the end of her eccentric but powerful message, she asked anyone who needed a miracle to stand. Cherith and I didn't hesitate. We stood to our feet.

"Ask now!" Heidi cried. "Whatever it is, there is grace here for breakthroughs."

We both looked at each other.

Neither of us needed to say a word.

We both started to weep.

And we uttered one sentence, "Miracles with Mark's children, Lord. Please, do miracles."

Within two months, two of my sons had reconnected with me. I had honestly thought, in my worst moments, they might never want to speak with me again. Someone had said just a few months before that his sons were still not speaking to him over twenty years after his divorce.

But God heard our sighs and saw our tears.

I met both sons.

I said sorry.

They forgave me.

We hugged and cried.

I was utterly speechless at their mercy and God's goodness.

My sons and I have been meeting and talking ever since. Not about my fall or my failures. That's forgiven. Everything else but those things.

Never forget.

Tears have immense power.

The sigh of our hearts is the best prayer we will ever pray.

When we get in touch with our grief, in a safe place with safe people, the prayer that rises up from our hearts ascends to the Father's heart in heaven.

When the two make contact, it is only a matter of time.

Help is on the way!

Cherith Adds

In the haze of our rebellion, I failed to see the hurt I had caused others. Perhaps it was denial. Perhaps it was a form of self-protection because I wasn't ready to take responsibility for what I had done. It was as if I was living in a parallel universe where I was simply unable to feel the remorse that, deep down, I knew I should be feeling.

The day Mark and I decided to go our separate ways, I felt heartbreak like I had never done before, but beneath it all, I had no doubt that, finally, we were doing the right thing. The floodgates had opened.

The first step was to own my decision and admit where – and why – I had gone wrong. Over the next few months, the haze began to lift and my grief poured out.

Repentance came in stages. After some weeks, my numbness began to ebb away and I began to feel again. I started to own my mistakes and apologise to those I'd hurt. I was able to apologise to some of the people I loved, who stood by me through it all.

Among those people were my parents. My mother is known as someone who says what she thinks and believe me, she doesn't hold back! Mum and I had many difficult conversations in that period. I know it cost her dearly to stand by me, when what I had done was so opposite to her beliefs, but stand she did.

I may not have agreed with everything she said – and she told me often she didn't agree with me – but I listened. I listened because she had earned the right to speak into my life at that deep level. She gave birth to me, nurtured me, and loved me unconditionally. I trusted her, so I listened.

Mum and Dad were uncompromising in their beliefs, but

they were also unwavering in their love and loyalty. That is an exceptionally difficult tightrope to walk and, as followers of Jesus, I believe we could all be better at it.

Repentance is not a 'Get out of jail free card'. It does not take away the consequences of our actions. It often goes hand-in-hand with tears and heartache. But what we experience the other side of that repentance is beautiful.

And it is worth it.

The longer you live in the pigpen, the more comfortable you become with the dirt that surrounds you. When you gain the courage to step out of the pigpen, and you begin to wash off the filth, you will wonder how you managed to survive there at all. There is hope for you.

You can do it.

God has not given up on you.

"Always pray and never give up" (Luke 18:1, NLT).

In a way, failure is a beautiful thing because, when the dust settles, there's nowhere to go but up. And it's a freedom.^{xx}

David Lynch
Film Director

9

THE SPEED OF GRACE

Sometimes it hits you when you least expect it. Not when you're up, but when you're down. Not when you're on the mountaintops, but in the valleys. Not when you're preaching up a storm, but when you're in the midst of a storm. Not when you're crowned with success, but scarred by failure. Then it strikes you. The outrageously and otherworldly love of God for broken, messed up people. His amazing grace. His scandalous kindness. The subversive, counter-cultural mercy of the Kingdom of heaven here on earth.

When I was at my lowest, numbed by the shock of my fall but desperate for reconnection with my Father, I sat in the office of Bill Johnson. That afternoon, as I sat with Bill, I had one of those moments when grace hits you like a wave. God was truly in his house that day.

I had just finished answering some questions that Bill had been asking about my life, telling my story as truthfully as I could, giving voice to my desperation for God's presence. He listened attentively, without censure or judgment. He then asked if he could pray for me. I nodded. This is what he said:

First of all, he quoted from my favourite book in the Bible, The Gospel of John (4:35-36):

Don't you have a saying, 'It's still four months until harvest'? I tell you, open your eyes and look at the fields! They are ripe for harvest. Even now the one who reaps draws a wage and harvests a crop for eternal life, so that the sower and the reaper may be glad together.

He then gave me a prophetic word about my restoration.

"People are saying that this will take a long time. It's going to be four months, four years, four decades. But I say to you, lift up your eyes. It's happening now."

I was stunned.

Somewhere, deep within the recesses of my mind, I had come to believe a lie. That lie came from the very heart of darkness, and went something like this: *Your restoration is going to take many years, perhaps even the rest of your life. And even if it is ever deemed to be complete, that still won't be good enough. Many will still judge you as worthless. Many will disqualify you from ministry, and permanently. You are going to die and people will always refer to you as 'the disgraced Mark Stibbe'.*

As soon as Bill gave his word, that lie was shattered. I suddenly knew with absolute certainty that the speed of grace can be very fast when human hearts are ready. Just as the disciples in John 4 needed to understand how God moves quickly in revival, so I needed to understand the same in relation to restoration. When God's on the move, things accelerate.

I even remember Bill saying later that I should come to Bethel the following year and speak at their writer's conference. My good friend Paul Manwaring – who was sitting with us in the office – rightly stepped in and said, "I think it might be a little early for that!"

Sometimes, when it comes to timing, the prophetic and the practical don't always line up perfectly!

Nonetheless, even if I was not ready to be invited to speak at Bethel, I was ready to accept that my idea of the speed of my restoration and God's idea might not be perfectly lined up either.

A few months later, Bill stood up at a conference in Harrogate. I was present in the audience, and was about to have dinner with him in a local restaurant. I was listening keenly.

During his talk, he deplored the way the Church puts religious demands on fallen people, stipulating that they should not be allowed back into ministry for three or four years minimum, even when they have clearly repented and been through a restoration process. In the culture of heaven, he said, things are very different.

It's All About Timing

The speed of restoration fascinates me. How long should it take for a person to be restored to ministry, if they have been evidently restored to relationship with God? Should it be another three to four years? Or should it be three to four minutes?

In *kintsugi*, the restoration of a broken cup, jar, or pot takes as long as it needs to take. There is no set time. The *kintsugi* artists know this. First, they have to wait until the *urushi* lacquer is ready. That takes as long as it needs to take. Everything depends on the conditions there and then. You cannot generalise about these things. It will be ready when it's ready.

Secondly, once the adhesive is ready, and it has been applied to the cracks, the teacup, jar or pot needs to be held together by rubber bands and then left to set in a space where there is both heat and water. Once again, there is no set time for this stage. Every *kintsugi* master knows that the object could be ready in a week or a month. It will be what it will be. You can neither move too fast, nor too slowly.

Thirdly, once the curing process is complete, the object needs to be inspected carefully to see if there are any rough edges. If there are places where protruding lacquer needs to be removed, the artist takes sandpaper or a razor and carefully makes the surface of the whole object as smooth as possible. Once again, this pain-staking process takes time. How long? That depends on how much excess dried lacquer needs to be shaved off the piece. It's all about timing, and things will be as they will be.

In a sense, *kintsugi* is all about time. It is an expression of the melancholic truth that all things decay, which is why objects repaired using the *kintsugi* method have always traditionally been displayed in a householder's tearoom during the first two weeks of autumn; the time of year in which the leaves fall off the trees, the colours begin to fade and animals prepare for hibernation. This is a period of time known as *Nagori*, in which the Japanese people keep a respectful and serene silence before the onset of winter – a silence in which failure, loss and brokenness is honoured and regarded as worthwhile because of the gold that shines in the cracks.

A Springtime Restoration

Of course, we mustn't expect everything about *kintsugi* to be the same as what we find in the Kingdom of heaven. In God's Kingdom, we don't see the decay of all things and simply accept this as the way things will always be. Yes, everything is in a state of decay. The Apostle Paul says as much, and he blames this on the Fall of humankind in the Garden of Eden. In Romans 8:19-21, Paul says:

> All creation is waiting eagerly for that future day when God will reveal who his children really are. Against its will, all creation was subjected to God's curse. But with eager hope, the creation looks forward to the day when it will join God's children in glorious freedom from death and decay.

The whole of creation is in decay because of the Fall. That Fall, in which Adam and Eve sinned, is one in which every human being shares. We are all fallen people and there is therefore no cause for pride. But the difference is this: Jesus has come into the world to reverse the curse of the Fall. Now creation is filled with living hope, not melancholic despair.

What is this hope? That one day all creation will move from fall to restoration. What is the source of this hope? It is the realisation within nature that the adopted sons and daughters of God are being forever taken on a journey from Fall to Restoration, death to life, decay to renewal.

Perhaps this is why, when Jesus comes to restore Peter on the shores of Galilee, he does so during the weeks after his death and resurrection, in the timeframe between Passover and Pentecost. In heaven's version of *kintsugi*, restoration takes place as nature springs to life again, not when it is decaying. One day, the Church may realise this and welcome back each Easter those who have been restored!

Accelerated Grace

One of the things that I have always loved about revivals is the way things happen quickly. More sinners get saved and restored in a few months than they have in decades. Sick people are healed quickly, instantly even. The demonised are set free in a moment, not after long nights and weeks of protracted prayer ministry.

In the books I have written about revival, I have used the phrase 'accelerated grace' to describe the way in which things that normally take a long time happen very quickly. When human hearts are ready, and when God is moving supernaturally, there is an acceleration as divine urgency meets human urgency.

This is true of restoration as well.

When human hearts are genuinely repentant.

When they are filled with a growing spiritual hunger.

When they long for an encounter with Jesus.

Then springtime comes to the fallen man or woman, just as it does to the Church in times of revival.

And it comes quickly. Very quickly.

Look at Simon Peter. He was genuinely repentant. He was spiritually hungry. He was longing to see Jesus again. When Peter told Jesus that he loved him more than anything, Jesus restored him.

How quickly?

In the time it took between verses 15 and 19 of John 21!

In verse 15 we read:

> After breakfast Jesus asked Simon Peter, "Simon son of John, do you love me more than these?"

In verse 19, Jesus tells Peter, "Follow me."

How long is that?

A matter of minutes.

That's all!

And that's outrageous!

Do you see how radically different the kindness of heaven is from the sternness of religion?

Religion says: "It's going to take a very long time, many years in fact."

Heaven says: "It's going to take as long as it takes, and that could be minutes."

When God moves supernaturally, you're no longer subject to and bound by the conventional passing of time. For him, a thousand years is like a day. Transformation can happen really quickly.

Gradually and Suddenly

That said, we must understand that God sometimes moves slowly. He doesn't always act suddenly.

That God acts suddenly is not in doubt. There are many examples of this in the Bible, in Church history and indeed in my own life. The greatest of all is the Day of Pentecost in Acts 2:1-4:

> When the day of Pentecost came, they were all together in one place. Suddenly a sound like the blowing of a violent wind came from heaven and filled the whole house where they were sitting. They saw what seemed to be tongues of fire that separated and came to rest on each of them. All of them were filled with the Holy Spirit and began to speak in other tongues as the Spirit enabled them.

Sometimes the Holy Spirit moves suddenly, as he did on the Day of Pentecost. We love these sudden interventions of heaven on earth. They make great stories. They make exciting testimonies. "I was healed immediately" sounds a whole lot more dramatic than "I was slowly healed over a period of five years".

But this does not mean that the Holy Spirit does not sometimes move more gradually. Nor does it mean that he places less value on the gradual. In Ezekiel 47:3-6, the river of God (a symbol of the Holy Spirit) moves out from the Temple and into the desert in stages:

> As the man went eastward with a measuring line in his hand, he measured off a thousand cubits and then led me through water that was ankle-deep. He measured off another thousand cubits and led me through water that was knee-deep. He measured off another thousand and led me through water that was up to the waist. He measured off another thousand, but now it was a river that I could not cross, because the water had risen and was deep enough to swim in—a river that no one could cross. He asked me, "Son of man, do you see this?"

I am tempted to ask: "Do you see this? Do you see how the Holy Spirit moves gradually? Do you see how the Spirit does not always come in the form of a flash flood? Do you see how sometimes the Spirit produces a rising tide in our lives – ankle deep, then knee high, waist high, then over our heads?"

The truth is, sometimes the issues in our hearts go so far back in our history, and so deep too, that a sudden deliverance would be all too much for us. Sometimes we need to be restored gradually, over time and in stages, so that the process doesn't overwhelm us. As God promised his people in Exodus 23:29-30:

I will not drive them out in a single year, because the land would become desolate and the wild animals too numerous for you. Little by little I will drive them out before you, until you have increased enough to take possession of the land.

If we are to be grown-up sons and daughters of God, we must learn to honour those times when our Father does things 'little by little', not just the more sensational moments when he does things 'suddenly'.

The Role of Counselling

If I'm right when I say that the Christian life is one long journey of inner healing, punctuated by moments of deliverance, then we need to do two things if we are to experience true and lasting restoration.

Firstly, we must renounce the false teaching that says emotional or inner healing is either unnecessary or demonic. That is sheer foolishness of the worst kind. In my experience, churches that neglect or despise Christian counselling are all too often led by people who most need it. Such people construct a theology that acts as a levy, a sea wall, against the love of God reaching the wounds of their hearts. Fear lies behind this – a terror of confronting the deep-rooted pain lodged within the soul, a fear of being vulnerable, a fear of being disapproved of or regarded as weak. All this is highly toxic. If people only realised how tender and loving our Father is, especially when he heals our hearts, we would be healthier and holier and our churches would be much safer places.

So my first encouragement, if it is needed, is to develop a more holistic Kingdom theology and to see the healing of your heart as a priority. If you don't, your life may end up in chaos. What would you rather do – have a regular MOT to expose and deal with faults, or wait until you have a car crash and confront those faults when it is too late?

This relates to my second encouragement: receive Christian counselling if you need it. A great deal of chaos and suffering could have been averted had I received Christian counselling over the years. In my restoration, I had two years of counselling with an amazing counsellor called Lynne. There, I confronted two major fault lines in my life: wounds from my mothers (my birth mother and my adoptive mother) and mother figures, and wounds from my boarding school days. If I had received counselling for these issues in my twenties as opposed to my fifties, it would almost certainly have prevented my fall. I simply cannot overstate the importance of Christian counselling. Please make sure you have that regular MOT so that you don't end up in a car wreck.

Finding the Sports Button

My restoration took time. Two years, to be precise, in which every fortnight I drove in my car the two hours to Derby and then met with my counsellor, Lynne. Within that process, I travelled to Bethel Church in California, met with Dawna De Silva, and had an encounter with Jesus.

I'm a 'both-and' kind of guy, not an 'either-or' one. I believe in both the suddenly and the gradually, the process and the crisis, the long journey of inner healing as well as the lightning strikes of deliverance.

You need wonderful counselling. But you also need the Wonderful Counsellor. It's 'both-and'. Sessions with a counsellor, and encounters with THE Counsellor; the Wonderful Counsellor, the Prince of Peace.

When I arrived at San Francisco Airport in May 2013, I went to pick up my hired car to drive to Redding.

"I'm afraid your car is no longer available," the agent said.

My heart sank.

"We're going to have to upgrade you at no extra cost."

My heart smiled.

"To a brand new, bright white BMW 6 Series sports car."

My heart skipped.

"Is that all right, sir?"

"It is," I replied.

A few minutes later, I was driving out of San Francisco.

On the long journey to Redding, I found myself on a freeway. At one point, it was practically deserted. It was like one of those movies where all you see is tumbleweed blowing across the tarmac.

All of a sudden, I noticed a button below me to my right with the word 'SPORT' on it. For about half an hour, I resisted the temptation to press it. But then I succumbed. When the road ahead and behind was clear, both sides of the central reservation, I pushed down on the sport button.

Nothing could have prepared me for what happened next.

The satnav changed from a map to an outline of the vehicle. On the screen a red, throbbing light started to appear in parts of the engine and throughout the car.

Then I heard a roar. In fact, I felt it, as the car moved effortlessly and powerfully from about 60 mph to 130 mph, in a matter of a few seconds.

I was thrilled for a moment. Then terrified.

My mind was filled with images of police helicopters and cars converging on me, blue lights flashing, officers emerging, their guns pointed towards me.

How was I going to slow down?

Eventually I figured it out, pressed the 'SPORT' button again, and the car decelerated. The image of the car with its heat-red engine disappeared from the screen, and the map returned.

The car returned to its normal speed.

And so did my heart.

The Divine Mechanic

The next day, I stood in Dawna's office, and as she prayed with me, in my mind's eye, I saw Jesus dressed as a car mechanic, bending over the opened bonnet or hood of a car, moving his hands at supernatural speed, fixing and improving the engine.

I sensed immediately that the car was my life and the engine was my heart.

As he finished, he shut the hood and wiped his oily hands on a rag.

There was a smile on his face.

The next moment, I saw that that same car outline again – the computerised image on the satnav monitor from the previous day. It was white, as it had been before I pressed the 'SPORT' button in the BMW on the freeway.

Then it changed.

That red, pulsating light appeared again.

I heard and felt a roar within me.

And a single word appeared before my eyes.

'ACCELERATION'.

In the thirty minutes of prayer that followed, I received more healing than in the previous thirty years.

Two years of wonderful counselling followed with Lynne.

But the whole process was kickstarted with a 'suddenly' – a

moment of miraculous healing in the presence of the Wonderful Counsellor.

Don't limit God.

If you open up your heart, the speed of grace is going to be faster than you could ever think or imagine.

Cherith Adds

Generally, I am much more cautious than Mark. It might take me three months to decide which washing machine we should buy, after hours of research about the best option. I am meticulous – some may say obsessive! Mark, on the other hand, walks into the store and comes out approximately 45 seconds later having purchased exactly what we needed. Job done.

It was a similar story when it came to our restoration. Within the process of his restoration, Mark experienced a series of 'suddenlys', whereas my journey was more slow and steady. We both arrived at the same place. It's just that God knew which route was best for each of us to take.

We are all wired uniquely, so don't expect everything to follow exactly the same course. It will look different for you. It will look different again for your friends. Be open to a 'suddenly', but try not to be frustrated if it doesn't happen. If someone in your world is moving towards repentance, it is not your responsibility to push them. Your role is to be there, to listen and to help them when their heart is ready.

God's grace and kindness can come from anywhere, and at any time. In those few months before Mark and I made the decision to go our separate ways, we were living in a flat together. We had rent and bills to pay but neither of us were working. I applied for various jobs and after a few failed applications and one failed interview at a coffee shop, I spotted an advertisement for a role that was perfect for me. It was a job that incorporated my skillset and my passion perfectly, so I decided to apply.

I was lucky enough to be given an interview and even more fortunate to be given the position. I spent three years there and

I met some wonderful people, many of whom I now consider to be close friends.

Throughout the turbulence of my personal circumstances, that job was a constant in my life and I'm so grateful for my time there.

A few years later, the time had come for me to move on from this job. One day, before I left, I was talking to one of the people who had interviewed me. She told me that over seventy people had applied for my job, many with more years of experience than me and one who had worked in the office of a previous Prime Minister!

Up against people with those kind of credentials, it was a miracle I got the job.

If I hadn't been able to work, Mark and I would most likely have been forced to go our separate ways because of immense financial pressures. We wouldn't have been able to meet our monthly outgoings and who knows where we would have ended up? Instead, I was undone by kindness in the midst of rebellion and amazing grace ushered me closer to my heavenly Father and thus closer to repentance.

I still don't understand it, but God didn't wait for me to do the right thing before he decided to be kind to me. In the end, I did the right thing *because of* his kindness.

The way our heavenly Father deals with broken people is mysterious and counterintuitive because he undermines us with generosity and grace.

God knows what he is doing.

Trust him and his process, and all will be well.

I am brave. I am bruised. I am who I'm meant to be.
This is me![xxi]

The Greatest Showman

10

REFINING YOUR DESTINY

In the two years after my fall, I found myself in what I called 'Rubble Town'. I was living at Ground Zero, trying to rebuild my life during a time of intensive restoration. What I came to realise quite quickly was that I needed to get to know the real me. All I had really known was the 'religious me' – the version of myself fashioned by my religious culture. That, I soon came to see, was a mythical version of myself. The question in my heart was this: "Will the real Mark please stand up?"

At some stage during this process, I began to think about the life I'd led up to the point of my fall. I had been an ordained minister for 25 years by that stage and had been involved in leading four churches. I had written books when I found the time, usually on days off and holidays. One Christmas, when I was vicar of St Andrew's Chorleywood, I went into my office on Christmas Day afternoon. The whole building was wonderfully quiet and all the doors were locked. I started writing and only stopped for meals and evenings, right up until New Year's Day. I completed a whole book during that week: *The Father You've Been Waiting For*. Then the church reopened and I went back to being a vicar again on 2 January.

Looking back at Rubble Town, I realised that there was something I loved far more than 'ministry'. My father had been a friend of CS Lewis and had imparted to me a great passion for books. Inspired by his enthusiasm for literature, I won a senior scholarship to Cambridge University where I studied literature for three years. Having been awarded a double first, Dad now wanted me to become a lecturer there.

That never happened. Thanks to the influence of my highly religious culture, I went to theological college to train for the ordained ministry and did a second degree in theology. Desperate for the approval of religious mentors and peers, I set course for Christian ministry and became a curate (an assistant pastor) in a church in Nottingham, and then in Sheffield. On my days off I studied for a PhD, which was eventually published by Cambridge University Press as *John as Storyteller.*

In Rubble Town, I reflected on this and realised that theology and ministry were not, and could never be, my first love. Besides the obvious (namely, Jesus), my first love was writing, but I had only ever been able to write when I had squeezed it into my busy schedule on days off and during holidays. This was not good for me, for my marriage, or for my children.

One of the consequences of my fall was that I went back to my childhood and remembered what it was that made me feel alive. It was books and writing. Somewhere along the way I had lost this in the all-consuming demands of leading churches and speaking at conferences.

In the end, I came to see that in my former life (before my fall), I had been a public speaker who squeezed in a bit of writing. Now that I had a chance to review my life, I went right back to basics. I reconnected with my passion. Since then, I have become a fulltime writer who squeezes in a little bit of speaking.

This was the gift that living at Ground Zero gave to me. I experienced, in God's amazing grace, a rediscovery of my true identity and a redefinition of my destiny. I cannot tell you how liberating it is to know who I am and what I'm destined to do, especially now that I am in the second half of life. I count this as an astounding blessing. I really like the new me in Christ. I really enjoy being who I am. When I write, I feel my Father's pleasure. It is who he wants me to be, what he wants me to do. That is a glorious freedom, right there.

Broken and Brilliant

This is one of the great lessons we learn from *kintsugi*. There is a greater beauty in the repaired pot, with the cracks showing, than ever there was before.

How wonderful that is! All the while I was leading churches and speaking on stages at Christian conferences, I was so aware of what needed to appear perfect. There is a certain way of behaving in these contexts and I am ashamed to say I not only conformed, I performed. However real and vulnerable I tried to be – and I really did try – there was always a sense in my heart deep down that I was out of sync with the real me, that I was presenting a mask, that I was not truly free to be myself.

Then came my moral fall. There could be no pretending any more. Now people knew who and what I really was. I couldn't hide and I couldn't disguise the huge fractures in my soul. I had presented myself to the world as a man of iron, but now my life was a pile of shattered porcelain on the floor, ready to be swept up and thrown away, to be replaced by the next favourite performer in the Christian conference culture.

I didn't know it at the time, but God was at work, even in my frailty. He is the divine Potter. He was never going to throw me away. He was never going to reject or replace me. He is a good, good Father. He saw the meaning in my mess.

My Dad gathered up the pieces of my fragmented soul. He glued all the pieces of my life back together again, showcasing his amazing grace by putting his goodness on display with the priceless gold of his love, luminous in my fractures. This new me is both the same as the old me and different too. I am a broken man, yes, but his glory shines out from the mending he has done in the time spent resting in the fire of his love, lying down by the still waters of his everlasting *Shalom*.

Now I have found my true voice.

After a long period alone with the Father, simply being, I have received his healing – I am still receiving his healing – and the words are flowing.

Even in this book.

I have been writing for just over a week.

The words just keep flowing out of my heart and onto the page.

No planning.

Just writing.

Truly, after the rest, there is a new *oration*.

Restoration. Restoration of identity. Redefinition of destiny.

This is always the way with Dad.

Simon Peter's Story

Peter discovered this in his restoration by the Sea of Galilee. In his original call, Jesus had used a very distinctive metaphor to describe Peter's identity and destiny in the Kingdom of God. The episode is strikingly similar to Peter's restoration. In Luke 5:1-11, we read this:

> One day as Jesus was standing by the Lake of Gennesaret, the people were crowding around him and

178

listening to the word of God. He saw at the water's edge two boats, left there by the fishermen, who were washing their nets. He got into one of the boats, the one belonging to Simon, and asked him to put out a little from shore. Then he sat down and taught the people from the boat. When he had finished speaking, he said to Simon, "Put out into deep water, and let down the nets for a catch."

Simon answered, "Master, we've worked hard all night and haven't caught anything. But because you say so, I will let down the nets."

When they had done so, they caught such a large number of fish that their nets began to break. So they signalled their partners in the other boat to come and help them, and they came and filled both boats so full that they began to sink.

When Simon Peter saw this, he fell at Jesus' knees and said, "Go away from me, Lord; I am a sinful man!" For he and all his companions were astonished at the catch of fish they had taken, and so were James and John, the sons of Zebedee, Simon's partners.

Then Jesus said to Simon, "Don't be afraid; from now on you will fish for people." So they pulled their boats up on shore, left everything and followed him.

Can you see the similarities with Peter's restoration? In both stories, Jesus comes to the shore with the specific intention of meeting Peter. In both stories, Jesus captivates Peter through an abundant catch of fish. In both stories, Peter is convicted of his sin. In both stories, Jesus commissions Peter for his new destiny.

Except for one difference.

In Luke 5, Jesus calls Peter to be a fisherman in the Kingdom.

In John 21, he calls him to be a shepherd in the Kingdom.

Listen to what Jesus says to Peter after breakfast in John 21:15-17:

> Take care of my lambs.
> Take care of my sheep.
> Feed my lambs.

Let's not get distracted by the differences between caring and feeding, or between lambs and sheep for that matter. Let's focus instead on the difference in metaphors. Jesus calls Peter to be a fisherman at the start. Now he is calling him to be a shepherd. Why is this?

Shepherds and Hirelings

Let me share with you something I discovered when I wrote my PhD on John 18-19. There I showed that the background for Peter's restoration is in Jesus' famous picture about shepherds and hired hands in John 10:

> Very truly I tell you Pharisees, anyone who does not enter the sheep pen by the gate, but climbs in by some other way, is a thief and a robber. The one who enters by the gate is the shepherd of the sheep. The gatekeeper opens the gate for him, and the sheep listen to his voice.

The first thing to notice about this 'figure of speech', or word picture, is the location. Jesus is describing a sheepfold, or a sheep pen. The sheep are in the pen, which originally would have been a walled enclosure with a single gate for going in and out. The shepherd is the one who leads the sheep out of the pen to feed, and into the pen to sleep. He is a good shepherd, as we learn a few verses later, because he protects the pen. He stands at the gate to the fold. In fact, he is the gate. And he lays down his life for the sheep.

This is a picture with a hint of danger. Why? There are two reasons. The first is because thieves are trying to get into the pen to steal the sheep. The second is because the shepherd employs hired hands to help him, but these hired hands run away when thieves or wolves appear.

What's this got to do with Simon Peter's restoration? Everything. In John 18:1-11, the Temple guards head to the garden where Jesus is with his disciples. The one who leads the soldiers to this secret location is Judas. In John's Gospel, he is called a thief – exactly the same word that's used by Jesus in John 10 to describe the person who tries to attack the sheep. Jesus, however, stands at the entrance to protect the sheep, revealing that he is the Good Shepherd of John 10 who will do anything to keep them safe, even lay down his life. John 10 is therefore the background for this story.

Jesus is the Good Shepherd.

The disciples are the sheep.

Judas is the thief.

The garden is the sheep pen.

So what does that make Peter?

If we go back to John 10:12-13, Jesus provides the answer when he talks about another character:

> The hired hand is not the shepherd and does not own the sheep. So when he sees the wolf coming, he abandons the sheep and runs away. Then the wolf attacks the flock and scatters it. The man runs away because he is a hired hand and cares nothing for the sheep.

This is why Jesus changes the metaphor from being a fisherman to being a shepherd in John 21. This is why he tells Peter to feed and tend the sheep, the lambs, in the fold (the Church). One day, Peter is going to be the under-shepherd of the flock. One day, he is going to have to do what good shepherds do, lay down his life for the sheep. As Jesus says in John 21:18-19:

> Very truly I tell you, when you were younger you dressed yourself and went where you wanted; but when you are old you will stretch out your hands, and someone else will dress you and lead you where you do not want to go.

John adds this:

> Jesus said this to indicate the kind of death by which Peter would glorify God.

Evangelists and Pastors

In terms of the fivefold gifts of the Spirit mentioned in Ephesians 4:11-12, what Jesus is doing is giving greater definition to Peter's destiny. During his restoration, Peter learns that he is not just called to be an evangelist (a fisherman), he is also called to be a shepherd (a pastor). He is called to look after broken people.

Here's why it's so important that Peter experiences a refining of his destiny during his restoration.

If a church is led by an evangelist, there will be a great deal of understanding and compassion given to the brokenness of the lost. Lost people are sinners, so we expect them to have made mistakes. We expect to hear of moral falls. We expect to hear of darkness. When these repentant sinners share their testimony, the church rejoices at hearing about how it once was, because it so graphically describes how powerful the gospel is in changing lives.

But what happens when those same people, now a few years down the line, run into trouble again? Maybe their marriage falls apart, or they succumb to a secret addiction. What then? How does the church respond when it has a fisherman at the helm? Does it spend as much time with the fallen believer as it did with the lost unbeliever? Does it show as much kindness and commitment to the one who is inside the fold as it did when they were out lost in the hills? Does it spend as much energy healing them as it did rescuing them?

This, I believe, is why Peter has to become a shepherd, not just a fisherman. The best church leaders are people who not only bring lost sheep into the fold. They are people who care for and feed the sheep when they are in the fold, even when the sheep are reckless and foolish – as sheep tend to be. They are people who walk with the fallen because they have fallen too. They provide a culture of restoration, because they have been restored too.

And the best shepherds for this are those who are transparent, truthful and vulnerable, who do not wear masks and perform to the crowds, but who are real about their failures, and give permission for everyone to be authentic, because as Richard Rohr so rightly says, "You cannot heal what you at first do not acknowledge."

An Unusual Easter Day

Let me give you an example of what this looks like.

A number of years ago, I went to speak at a church in the USA. The African American pastor met me at the airport and drove me to his city.

On the way, he started talking about his personal problems. He obviously felt safe to do so. We were both men, both alone, both committed to being real.

"I've been addicted to pornography since I was 13," he said with a sigh. "No one knows except my wife. And I'm leading a church, man."

"What help have you had?" I asked.

"I've tried everything. I've repented time and time again, but that hasn't stopped it. I've received deliverance at least twice, and that hasn't stopped it. I just can't break free and I'm desperate."

"What has your relationship with your mother been like?" I asked.

He paused, staring ahead at the road.

Then he began to speak.

"I've never thought of that. To be honest, it was great until I was 13. We were really close. But when I grew up physically, I started to look and sound like my Dad, and she just rejected me. It was never the same after that."

"In my experience," I said, "people in your situation deal with the fruit but not the root of their addiction."

"What do you mean?"

"I mean that we repent of the acts and we try to get rid of the demons, but all the while the thing at the core of this habit remains."

"And what's that?"

"With men, it's often a mother wound. Men seek for the solace they miss from their mothers through toxic attachments. Missing the nurturing love of a mum, they seek out the breast of another. It's really common."

At that moment, the lights came on in my friend's head.

"That's it!" he cried. "I have a mother wound that needs healing."

And he received it, right there and then, in the car!

Three days later, on Easter Sunday morning, my friend stood up in front of his church and confessed everything. He told his church family that he had been healed. Then he asked anyone who had a secret problem in this or a related area to come forward. Two thirds of the people came to the altars that day for forgiveness and healing!

Now that is church.

That is what I mean by being real. And being real is the path to being healed.

Nothing is gained by presenting the illusion of perfection to a congregation. This just keeps people in game-playing mode, presenting a *faux* righteousness to each other. But when leaders are vulnerable, when leaders are transparent about their falls and failures, and when leaders talk about where they have found keys to supernatural restoration, it gives permission for everyone to do the same.

Today, eight years later, my friend is still completely free!

He is a work of *kintsugi* art, more beautiful for the golden cracks than ever he was when he was performing, striving, to look perfect.

Out of the Wreckage

My own fall had very painful consequences, especially for those nearest and dearest to me, and this is something I deeply regret. But I decided early on that I wanted to be positive, to learn what lessons I could, resolving never to making the same mistake again. It was for that reason that I not only received counselling, I also received regular prayer for inner healing and deliverance.

In every plane crash, aviation experts search for the black box recorders so that they can learn everything they need to about why things went wrong. They deal with these issues transparently and meticulously, resolved to publish their findings so that necessary changes can be made throughout the aviation industry to prevent similar crashes occurring again. Matthew Syed talks about this in his book *Black Box Thinking*. His message is clear: Be very honest about what's gone wrong, and then harness the experience of failure in a positive way. Not just in the aviation industry either, but in every walk of life.

In Rubble Town, one of the many lessons I learned was that the days of pretending are now over. I am no longer going to perform in order to earn people's approval. All that is orphan behaviour and, as I wrote earlier in this book, my fall gave me a choice: whether to blame others, as an orphan does, or to grow up and take responsibility, as mature sons and daughters do. I chose the latter and in the process experienced a refining of my sense of identity (the real me) and my destiny (my true purpose).

I now regard my time in Rubble Town as a gift. It's tough there, really tough, and I wouldn't recommend anyone going there by choice. But it was there that I recalled a time in the 1980s when I had been at a John Wimber conference and my right hand had started shaking, my writing hand. God had told me then and there that I was to be a writer in his Kingdom.

I remembered a time twenty years later when Stacey Campbell called me to stand during a conference. She prophesied that I was a modern day Augustine, called to write my own version of the *Confessions* and the *City of God*.

I then recalled how ten years later I had been due to speak at Toronto Airport Christian Fellowship when a woman who did not know me prophesied over me that I was going to move from non-fiction to fiction and write novels.

Suddenly, I realised that I had lost a sense of who I was. It wasn't that the ministry had been unproductive. It was simply that it wasn't the real me. Now it was time to get back to my identity and destiny, and to experience the convergence of my passion and purpose.

The Hardest Battle

Peter went through a moral failure and restoration, but on the far side of this arduous process he came to a truer sense of who he was and what he was called to do. He was called to be a loving shepherd to vulnerable sheep. To do that, he needed to embrace not only the agony of being broken, but also the ecstasy of being restored. This then made him authentic and real as a leader. As one friend said to me after my restoration, "I think it's important that we never follow a man without a limp." Peter, like Jacob of old, now had a limp. He had been emptied of his self-confidence and filled with a new and humble reliance on his Father. That cockiness (if you'll pardon the pun) was never to come back. Now he was who he was truly meant to be.

Here's my advice. Discover and implement these things without having to go through Rubble Town. This is not narcissism, as someone once charged me. It is being human. It is obeying the ancient Greek dictum, "Know Yourself". It is learning to love and like yourself before it's too late, before the plane crashes.

The American poet E.E. Cummings once said this:

To be nobody but yourself in a world which is doing its best day and night to make you like everybody else means to fight the hardest battle which any human being can fight and never stop fighting.[xxii]

Two years before my fall, I kept hearing this one statement over and over again in my heart. "I am going to dismantle you, my son. Then I am going to re-mantle you."

I had no idea what that meant at the time, but after my restoration I knew.

I needed dismantling.

There were wounds lodged so deep – wounds of abandonment and abuse – that only something drastic was going to cause me to face them.

There were aspects of my ministry and work that were so out of alignment with my identity and destiny, that only something dramatic would make me take the risk to ask tough questions, only something traumatic would give me the courage to change course so radically.

But that was not the end.

After the dismantling comes the re-mantling.

What that looks like, I don't fully know yet.

But I'm excited.

Really excited.

Because I know it's going to be real this time round.

And that for me is everything, because as my favourite author Brennan Manning once wrote, "in Love's service, only wounded soldiers can serve."

Or, to use the *kintsugi* analogy, in heaven's tearoom, only broken teacups are put on display.

Please, Just Lie Down!

So then, after the *rest* comes the *oration*. After Peter's time of solitude, he was given a seat again at the table, and he was given a voice again. His voice would be different now. It would be less cocksure (pardon the pun again). Less self-assured and self-reliant. More humble. More authentic. More dependent on the Father's infinite resources. When his time for *oration* came, he would stand up on the Day of Pentecost and speak with a tongue on fire! To do this, he had needed time out and healing.

Sometimes, we are so busy ministering for God that we forget to simply receive his ministry for ourselves. This is what *rest* does. It positions us to hear Jesus gently telling us where our hearts need healing, where our lives need realigning. Like Moses, sometimes we have to stop performing in the palace and head to the desert for some time alone, tending the sheep and running into burning bushes. If we took the time and the trouble to rest and listen on a regular basis, we would almost certainly avoid the crises that force us to lie down and listen.

In this chapter we have been talking about shepherds, so it is only right at this point to mention Psalm 23. We are so familiar with these words that we are apt to miss their significance:

> The Lord is my shepherd, I lack nothing. He makes me lie down in green pastures, he leads me beside quiet waters, he refreshes my soul.

Did you see it?

He *makes me lie down*.

Who does?

The shepherd.

Where?

In green pastures.

Why?

To refresh my soul.

My SOUL!

That part of me where the uniqueness of who I am is contained. That part of me which is composed of all my memories, my experiences, my history – right back to the time of my conception. It is the part of me that thinks, reasons, analyses, reflects, considers, imagines, and dreams. It is that part of me that feels all the emotions that human beings experience, from fear to love and back again. It is the story-shaped centre of my life, and that story is uniquely and eternally my own.

This is the part of me that my heavenly Father wants to refresh. He wants me to spend time in the long grass under the sun, chewing the corn and listening to the rustling of the stalks in the breeze. He wants me to hear his gentle whispering as he shines his divine light on areas of my soul that are fractured and sinful, because he wants me to receive his healing and his refining. He wants me blameless and he wants me holy. Only when I stop and rest can I receive this therapeutic and transformational refreshment.

And if the Good Shepherd can't woo us to embrace such moments, the Psalmist says that he will *make us lie down in green pastures*. He will allow life circumstances to lead us into enforced rest so that we can lie on his couch and receive the matchless ministry of heaven's Wonderful Counsellor, our Prince of *Shalom*.

And the Psalmist knew this.

Because the Psalmist was King David.

David experienced a moral fall.

He went through a process of restoration.

In the rest, he experienced healing and he experienced refining.

But after the *rest* came the *oration*.

His voice was released again.

And this time, his voice was sweeter, richer, deeper, kinder, truer, more poetic than ever before.

Finding your Voice

For me, the years I spent almost entirely on my own were extraordinarily important. During that season, the Lord made me lie down in green pastures. He made me listen. He made me attentive.

During these times of refreshing, he began to show me things about myself that I had never seen before. He revealed the mother wounds at the heart of my life – wounds that I had ignored. I had been so busy talking about father wounds that I had failed to see an even deeper, primal pain from my birth mother, my adoptive mother, and other mother figures in my life. Others had seen it. For example, my friend Lois Gott, on hearing of my moral fall, turned to her husband Ken and said, "That's Mark's mother wound." She wasn't excusing what I had done, she was pointing to something that I had failed to address.

Now I had to confront it. In fact, I spent the better part of two years receiving lasting freedom through both the counselling and through moments of inner healing and deliverance. God honoured both the sessions with my counsellor and those times of divine intervention. He refreshed my soul by adding his super to my natural!

All this released my voice. It enabled me to speak to others about these wounds and about how to find healing. In fact, it has led to a whole new teaching on healing from the wounds from our mothers.

This, in turn, has led to many, many others receiving the same mother-like comfort from God that I received as I lay down in green pastures and strolled beside still waters.

And this was not the only thing.

The long season of counselling and healing revealed another wound – one that had made a huge and destructive impact on my life. I had been sent away to boarding school on my eighth birthday. For the next ten years, I spent over three quarters of each year away from my parents and my home. Like countless others, I became what I call 'a boarding school orphan', living in what my friend Nicki Beaumont calls 'an orphanage for the privileged'. The effects of this ruptured attachment were devastating, but I had pushed the pain down and suppressed these memories for nearly fifty years.

Until I fell.

Then they began to surface.

Not giving me an excuse, but offering a reason.

And with the help of my counsellor Lynne, I received one revelation after another, one healing after another, until I was ready to share my story.

And that's what I did, in a book called *Home at Last,* about recovering from boarding school pain.

I have received hundreds of messages from people whose lives have been impacted and changed by the story I tell in that book, and the healing journey I describe in its pages. Just this week, I was deeply moved by the following remarks in an email from a lady I've never met before:

It is so amazing to discover, even at this late stage in my life, that there is help and support, possible healing and recovery from the most debilitating shame and anxiety that I have suffered for the last fifty years. Just reading Mark's book makes me realise that there is a root to all this, which I have never recognised before, just feeling guilty and ashamed as a Christian for all these feelings.

Just this week, I have received an invitation from a boarding school to come and speak to the staff about how to offer help and healing to pupils who are suffering from the trauma of separation from their families and homes.

God is good!

Truly, he makes us lie down in green pastures.

Truly, he refreshes our souls.

Truly, after the *rest*, comes the *oration*.

When we discover who we really are, then we discern what we are truly meant to do on this earth.

With our history healed and our identity sealed, it isn't long before our destiny is revealed.

And, as in Simon Peter's life, there will be no stopping the new, true you!

Cherith Adds

It means a lot when someone believes in you. It means everything when someone believes in you after you have messed up.

Before my fall, unlike Mark, I was not in the public eye. This doesn't mean that there was no rubber-necking, it just meant it was harder to do because I was under the radar – which, incidentally, is where I'm happiest!

In 2016, four years after our fall, Mark and I had each worked our way (separately) through a restoration process. In September that year, after we had got married, Mark was asked by one of our dearest friends, Pastor Theresa, to minister at her church in Rhode Island, USA.

When we arrived, Theresa picked us up from the airport. On the way to Rhode Island, she mentioned that I would be leading a small group of young women in breakout sessions over the weekend. I thought I was going to throw up! I knew God had forgiven me. I knew he loved me. But I wasn't sure if he really trusted me.

I hadn't ministered like this before my fall, when I felt qualified and capable (and honestly, a little bit pious), so how on earth was I going to do it now I was so broken?

The answer is in the question. Now, I was relying on God alone because I *knew* from experience he was all I had.

I couldn't believe that this American pastor, who knew my story well, would even consider me as an option.

That was my *kintsugi* moment.

Just a few months ago, we were back at that church in Rhode Island and after the service, I was handed this note:

Cherith,

I want to express my gratitude for all that you poured into my stepdaughter and our family during your last visit. It is hard to even put into words the profoundness of the impact you had because of your willingness to let the Lord use you with the group of teen girls you ministered to during your last visit. You have a sweet, gentle grace that spoke to them and nudged them closer to the Father. My daughter was changed by the experience – delivered of some of her hurt and forever changed – forever changing our family too.

Church, if we say we are family, then let's act like one. Choose to believe in those who are broken. Especially when they don't believe in themselves.

There is gold in your wounds.[xxiii]

Guillermo del Toro
Film Director and Storyteller

CONCLUSION

Being married to a Northern Irish wife is a constant learning curve. I have to understand phrases like 'clean foundered' (very cold), and references to the 'hot press' (the airing cupboard). Most of all, I have to become more and more aware of the difference between Irish social customs and my own. For example, when someone in Northern Ireland announces they are leaving, they get up and say goodbye, but thirty minutes later, they are still there! My conclusion now, from five years of experience, is this: when someone from Cherith's family says it's time to go, it really isn't.

This book is a bit like that. You probably thought I was signing off at the end of the last chapter. But I wasn't. Here I am, still typing away, even after you thought I'd said goodbye!

It's a bit like John's Gospel. You thought it was all over at the end of Chapter 20, but then John gives us another chapter about Peter's encounter with Jesus.

It's a bit like my life story. People thought it was all over when I fell. But it's not! I'm still here.

So, what's so important that I had to write a conclusion?

It's this:

Just when I thought I'd finished writing, I found out something about *kintsugi* that worried me. It was a part of the analogy that I had not considered or mentioned, but one that I realised straightaway I needed to include and discuss.

I discovered that after the *kintsugi* method was invented, Japanese people became so enamoured with the beauty of teacups repaired with golden joinery that they intentionally threw their cups and jars on the floor, just so that they could have them restored using *kintsugi*.

As soon as I saw that, I realised that there is something I need to add to this book before I finish.

So let me say this, and firmly.

Do not use our story as a license to do something that is intentionally designed to hurt yourself and others, just so that you can access the kind of insights we have been describing in this book.

We have purposefully written this book precisely in order to *prevent* you from going through what we've gone through. This book is a reason to get up again. It is not an excuse for falling.

No one should sin just to access more of God's grace. Paul makes it clear in Romans 6:1-2 that this is entirely misguided and extremely dangerous to our spiritual health. This is the Passion Bible Translation, by my friend Brian Simmonds:

> So what do we do, then? Do we persist in sin so that God's kindness and grace will increase? What a terrible thought! We have died to sin once and for all, as a dead man passes away from this life. So how could we live under sin's rule a moment longer?

The answer has got to be no!

So, if you're thinking of falling: don't do it, I implore you. Don't use our story as a template for your own. And don't fall just so you can experience *kintsugi* for yourself. You have no idea what you're asking for if you do. It's a death process for you and a lot of hurt for others. Pull back. Hold off. Talk to someone wiser and older than you. And get help.

If you're walking with a fallen friend or family member, please be kind, empathetic and non-judgmental. Make the Church a safer place for people to experience *kintsugi*. Cherith and I have been so appalled by the way many fallen people have been treated, even by their own family members. I have been deeply upset by the frequent comments made by people I know that the Church can be such a brutal place for those seeking restoration. As Billy Graham's grandson recently tweeted:

> I have hundreds of letters from people all over the world telling me their own crash and burn stories and they all reveal a sad common thread: the Christian community is all too often the scariest place for fallen people to fall down and for broken people to break down.

This was confirmed to me recently by an old friend who has recently gone through divorce and remarriage. He described to me how he, and many others like him, have found the Church to be an extremely inflammatory and dangerous environment. As he said to me on the phone just last week, "Too many lapsed or fallen believers don't even attempt to come back to church because they know they're going to be burnt up on re-entry."

That's tragic.

And it's a great waste of gifts and callings too.

So, be kind and be humble.

If your life is going well for you, don't look down on those who have fallen. As Teresa Wairimu Kinyanjui wrote, in a book that Cherith and I recently edited:

The Christian life is like riding a bicycle; when one peddle is up, the other peddle is down. The peddle that is up cannot boast to the peddle that is down, because soon they will exchange places. So then, bless me when I am up because I will pick you up, and when I am down you will pick me up.

Be humble. Pride comes before a fall.

Let's make the Church a safe place for broken people. Let's practice the Kingdom version of *kintsugi* and celebrate repaired teacups in the tearooms of our churches. Let's stop bowing down to the illusory perfection associated with performance and celebrity, and let's be real. Let's be like Jesus in John 21, and be kind.

And if you're a fallen man or woman, let me gently urge you to entrust the fragments of your shattered life to your Father, the divine Potter. Let him put the pieces back together again in his way and his time. Let him bring beauty out of your brokenness. Let him restore you, just as he did Peter in John 21. This is his purpose.

Remember King David? He went through the experience of a great fall, and a deep restoration. What was it he prayed during that time? Here's what David says in Psalm 51:13 (the Passion Bible Translation, again):

Then I can show to other guilty ones how loving and merciful you are. They will find their way back home to you, knowing that you will forgive them.

David's longing was not to waste anything, but to use his mistakes to help others.

What is the lesson here?

Use your experience of being broken and repaired by your loving Dad to guide other people home into his arms.

Jesus knew Peter was going to fall. This was no surprise or shock to him. But his prayer was that Peter would use his failure and harness the lessons from it in such a creative way that he could be a help to others. He told Peter that he was praying for good fruit after the fall. That's why he said, "make it your life mission to strengthen the faith of your brothers" (Luke 22:32, *Passion Bible Translation*).

Remember, most of all, the biggest lesson from *kintsugi*:

> *The restored pot, with its gold-covered cracks, is worth far more than the original, unblemished pot could ever be.*

That sounds like the Kingdom of heaven to us!

Not all who wander are lost.[xxiv]

J.R.R. Tolkien
Storyteller

THE MAN WHO RAN
A NOVEL
Mark Stibbe

A perfect, fictional accompaniment to
Restoring the Fallen

It's Christmas Eve and festive lights are guiding people home. Jake Graystone (44), however, is about to make the worst decision of his life. Bored by his job, and unable to provide for his wife and two sons, Jake has a chance meeting with an old school friend in a local bar.

Pete Marley (44) and Jake have known each other since university days. While Jake's life has plateaued, Pete is a poker champion and has everything. Three months before Christmas, Pete teaches Jake the art of poker. In the dimly lit bar, he whispers the secret of the cards.

Jake is now drawn into a world of gambling and Sally (39), his long-suffering wife, realises she is losing the man she loves.

Jake cannot keep his secret forever, however, and when his wife finds out, there is a volcanic argument on Christmas Eve.

Jake walks out on his family, gets into his car and heads north to Casino City with barely a thought for the people he is leaving behind.

He is entering a world of deep darkness. A world of addiction and crime. But a world in which angel feathers will touch his heart.

With themes familiar to readers of A Christmas Carol and The Parable of the Prodigal Son, this exquisitely written story is both heart-breaking in its rawness and heart-warming in its redemptive power.

Malcolm Down Publishing
July 2019

Sent away to boarding school on his eighth birthday, Mark Stibbe watched his adoptive parents drive down a gravel road, leaving him standing in front of a huge country house with his trunk and his teddy. That night, already confused and frightened, he was given the first of four beatings in his first two weeks. This trauma of abandonment and abuse was to scar Mark's life until his fifties, when divorce forced him to deal with he calls his 'boarded heart'. In this ground breaking book, Mark argues that there are many thousands of wounded people just like him, men and women who suffer throughout their lives with homesick souls. This often leads to them being driven to succeed in their work while failing to engage emotionally at home.

ISBN: 9781910786413
£10.99

Sarah Grace is a fully qualified psychotherapist who works extensively with former boarding school pupils and their families either one to one or during one-day retreats.

Sarah also runs a counselling network for referrals. If you are a therapist and would be interested in joining please email as below.

grace4counselling@gmail.com

Endnotes

i.   https://www.goodreads.com/work/quotes/4652599-a-farewell-to-arms

ii.   Sam Wallace, "How Gareth Southgate is using his own bitter failure to end England's penalty curse," *The Telegraph*, July 2, 2018.

iii. R J Palacio, *Wonder*, (London: Random House, 2014), 48.

iv.   Teresa of Avila. AZQuotes.com, Wind and Fly LTD, 2018. https://www.azquotes.com/quote/670599.

v.   Bill Bennot, https://twitter.com/bbennot/status/439278959357067264?lang=en.

vi.   Simon Burnton, "50 stunning Olympic moments No3: Derek Redmond and dad finish 400m," *The Guardian*, November 30, 2011.

vii. Henri Nouwen Quotes. BrainyQuote.com, BrainyMedia Inc, 2018. https://www.brainyquote.com/quotes/henri_nouwen_105224.

viii. Kenji Mizoguchi, *Ugetsu*. 1953; Japan: Umbrella Entertainment, 2016. DVD.

ix.   Theodore Roeke, *Straw for the Fire: From the Notebooks of Theodore Roethke*, ed. David Wagoner, (Washington: University of Washington Press, 1980), 179.

x.   Leonard Cohen Quotes. BrainyQuote.com, BrainyMedia Inc, 2018. https://www.brainyquote.com/quotes/leonard_cohen_156369.

xi.   Marcel Proust, *In Search of Lost Time*, (London: Penguin Classics, 2003).

xii. Richard Rolle, *The Fire of Love*, ed. Clifton Wolters, (London: Penguin Classics, 1972)

xiii. Ibid.

xiv. Brené Brown, *Daring Greatly: How the Courage to Be Vulnerable Transforms the Way We Live, Love, Parent, and Lead*, (New York: Penguin, 2012), 75.

xv. William Barclay, *Barclay on the Lectionary: Matthew, Year A,* (Edinburgh: St Andrew Press, 2013), 200.

xvi. Ulysses S. Grant Quotes. BrainyQuote.com, BrainyMedia Inc, 2018. https://www.brainyquote.com/quotes/ulysses_s_grant_132903.

xvii. Raymond Carver, *Late Fragment,* allpoetry.com, 2012. https://allpoetry.com/Late-Fragment

xviii. Paul Tillich, *The Shaking of the Foundations*, (Oregon: Wipf and Stock, 2012).

xix. http://www.metanoiaproject.co.uk/beone/ourfather/Thy%20Kingdom%20Come.pdf

xx. David Lynch and Kristine Mckenna, *Room to Dream*, (New York: Random House, 2018), 227.

xxi. Michael Gracey, The *Greatest Showman*. 2017; 20th Century Fox Home Entertainment, 2018. Blu-ray.

xxii. e. e. cummings Quotes. BrainyQuote.com, BrainyMedia Inc, 2018. https://www.brainyquote.com/quotes/e_e_cummings_161592.

xxiii. Guillermo del Toro, *The Shape of Water*. 2018; 20th Century Fox Home Entertainment, 2018. DVD.

xxiv. J. R. R. Tolkien, *The Fellowship of the Ring*, (London: HarperCollins, 2005), 170.